KINDERGARTEN MATH WORKBOOK

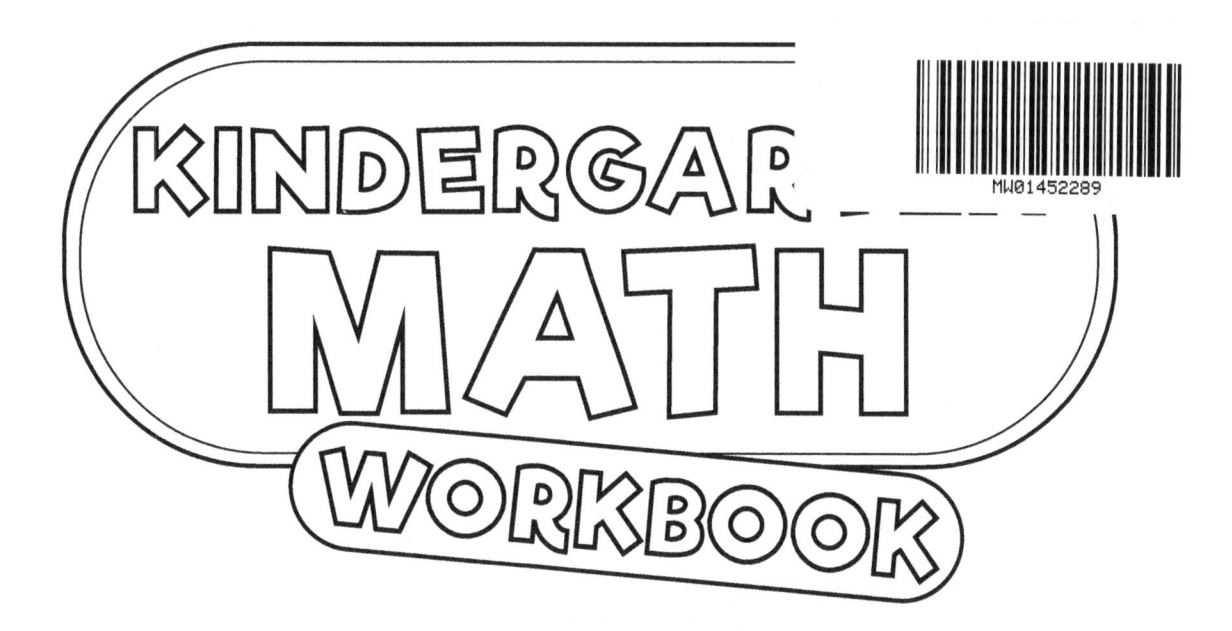

Thank you for trusting us with supporting your childs development. We've worked hard to get this addition right:

100 pages of kindergarten math activities
+
Fun challenges
=
A head start for your child.

This book is designed for kids to get a great understanding of early math, be confident using it and be school ready. We've built this workbook with a variety of math activities to give a broad foundation for kids ages 4-6.

As every child progresses differently, some concepts in the workbook will be familiar and can be used to strengthen existing skills. Other skills will be new and more challenging. We've structured the book in clear sections to allow children and parents to easily move between them, and to revisit or skip topics depending on need.

Throughout the book there are exercises for coloring, writing and drawing. A selection of coloring pens or pencils will be needed along with a pair of scissors for creating your own math flash cards on page 20!

We hope you and your little one enjoy this workbook and their journey of math learning!

© 2021 Under The Cover Press. All Rights Reserved.
www.UnderTheCoverPress.com

Contents

	Page
Writing numbers	2
Addition	5
Subtraction	12
Color by numbers	18
Create your own math flash cards	20
Number connect	27
Number lines	31
Skip counting	41
Number bonds to 10	45
Number bonds to 20	49
Color and count	53
Number patterns	58
Ordinal numbers	62
Shapes	66
More and Less	70
Odd and even	74
Left and right	77
Bigger and smaller	79
Longer and shorter	83
Whole and half	86
Telling the time	90
Challenges	94
Count to 100	101
Practice paper	102
Diploma	105

This

KINDERGARTEN MATH WORKBOOK

Belongs to

....

Writing Numbers

Practice tracing and then writing numbers. Start at the star!

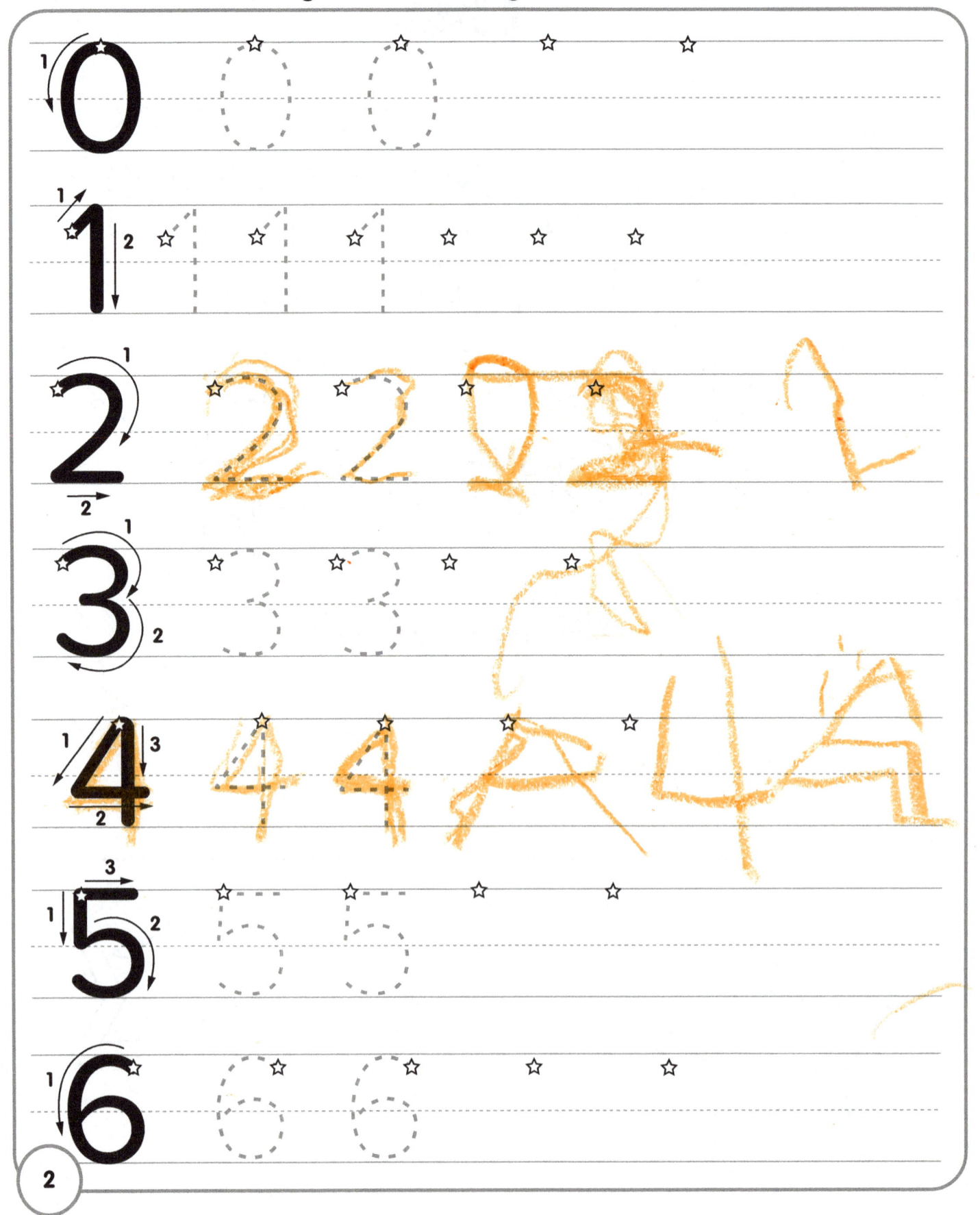

0
1
2
3
4
5
6

2

7 7 7
8 8 8
9 9 9
10 10

Combine your skills and the empty practice lines below to write these numbers. Start at the star!

18 13 20 11

Trace

18 13 20 11

Write

Write

Count the objects and write the number.

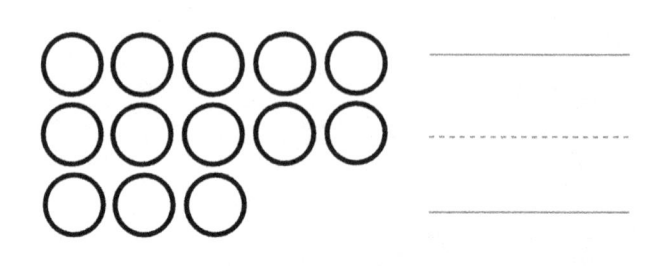

Here are mixed up numbers from 1 to 9, which number is missing?

4

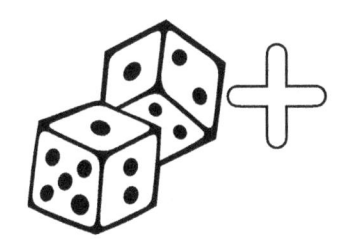

Addition

Add the numbers or objects together

Addition means adding numbers to other numbers to make a BIGGER number.

For example, if you had 4 donuts and you bought 3 more donuts, how many donuts would you have all together?

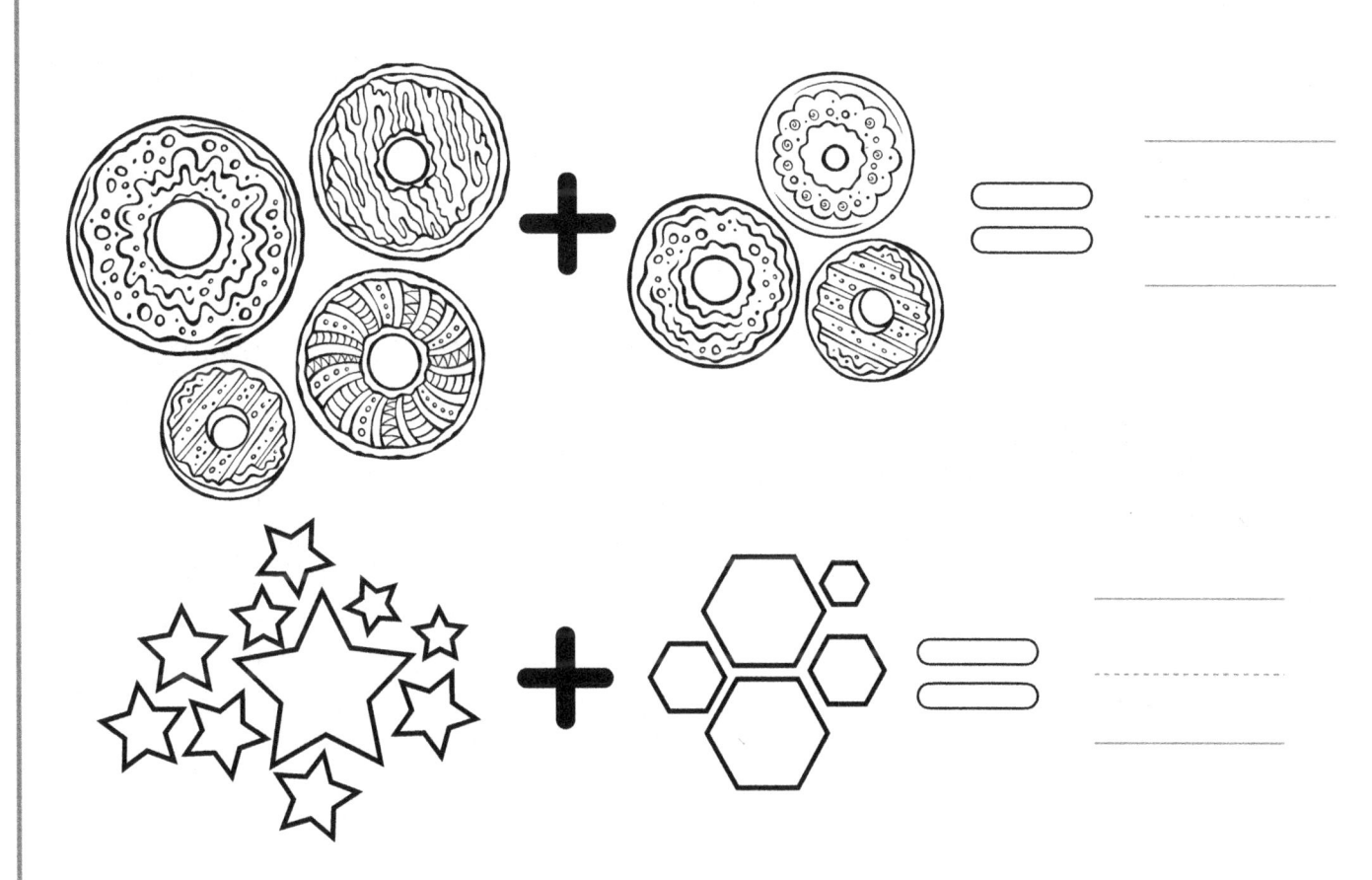

_____

[donuts] + [donuts] = _____

[stars] + [hexagons] = _____

We can use these 10 FRAMES to easily see and add numbers together. By counting and drawing the circles we can see the answer here.

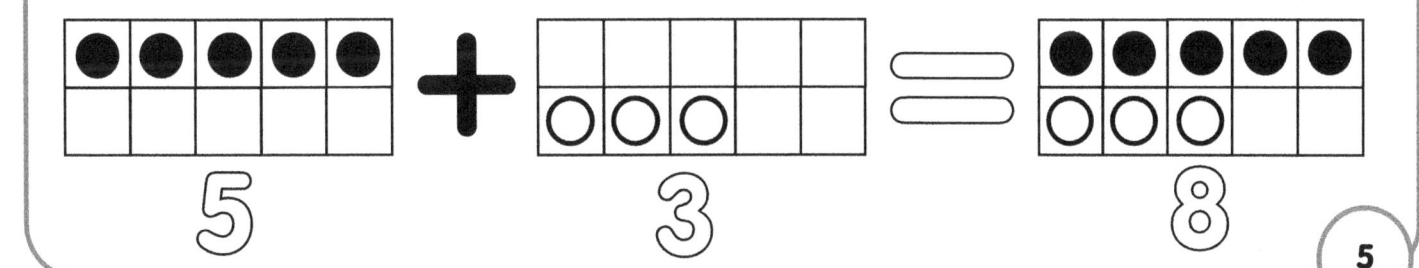

5 + 3 = 8

5

Use these 10 FRAMES to work out the answers.
Write the number of circles under each 10 FRAME and draw the circles to show the answer.

___ + ___ = ___

___ + ___ = ___

We can add bigger numbers too by adding extra 10 FRAMES!

___ + ___ = ___

___ + ___ = ___

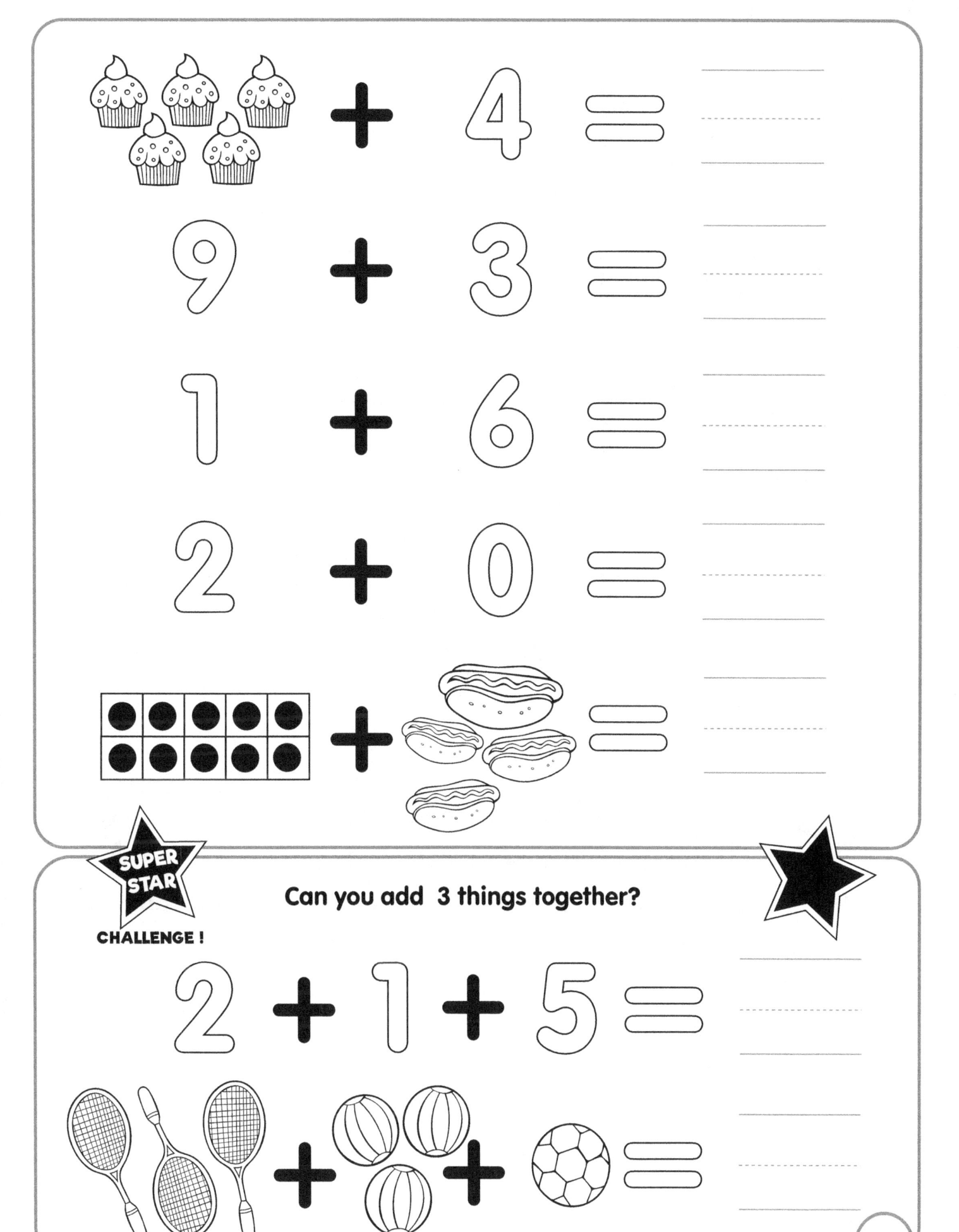

🧁🧁🧁🧁🧁 + 4 = _____

9 + 3 = _____

1 + 6 = _____

2 + 0 = _____

▦ + 🌭🌭🌭🌭 = _____

SUPER STAR CHALLENGE!

Can you add 3 things together?

2 + 1 + 5 = _____

🎾🎾🎾 + 🏐🏐🏐 + ⚽ = _____

7

3 + 12 = _____

14 + 6 = _____

🌞🌞🌞🌞🌞🌞 + 13 = _____

11 + 🎈🎈🎈🎈🎈🎈🎈🎈🎈 = _____

SUPER STAR CHALLENGE!

Make your own addition challenge!

① Color in any number of dots you like.
② Write the number of dots you've colored underneath.
③ Add the numbers together!

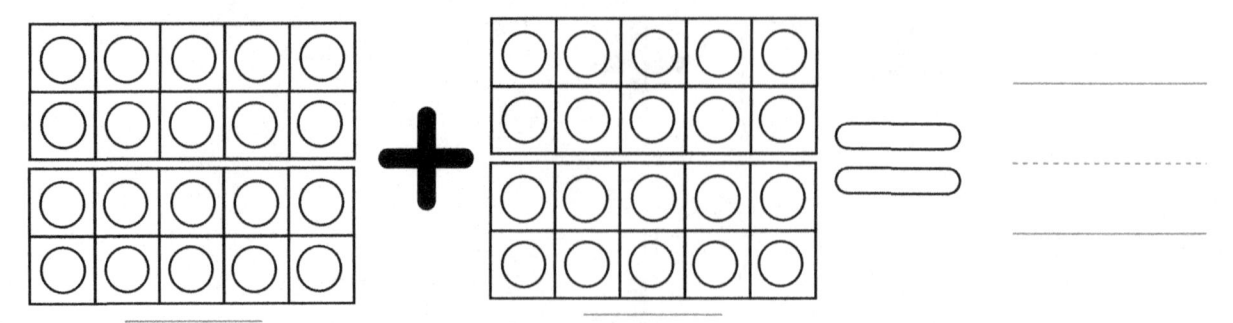

[ten-frame] + [ten-frame] = _____

_____   _____

8

We can also change the sums we need to solve!

5 + _____ = 8

_____ + _____ = _____

If you saw 6 butterflies in the field, then 2 more butterflies landed next to them, how many butterflies are there now?

If you have 11 pencils and you add 4 more, how many pencils are there now?

There are 9 cars in the parking lot. 5 more cars arrive. How many cars are now in the parking lot?

Try this mix of addition challenges!

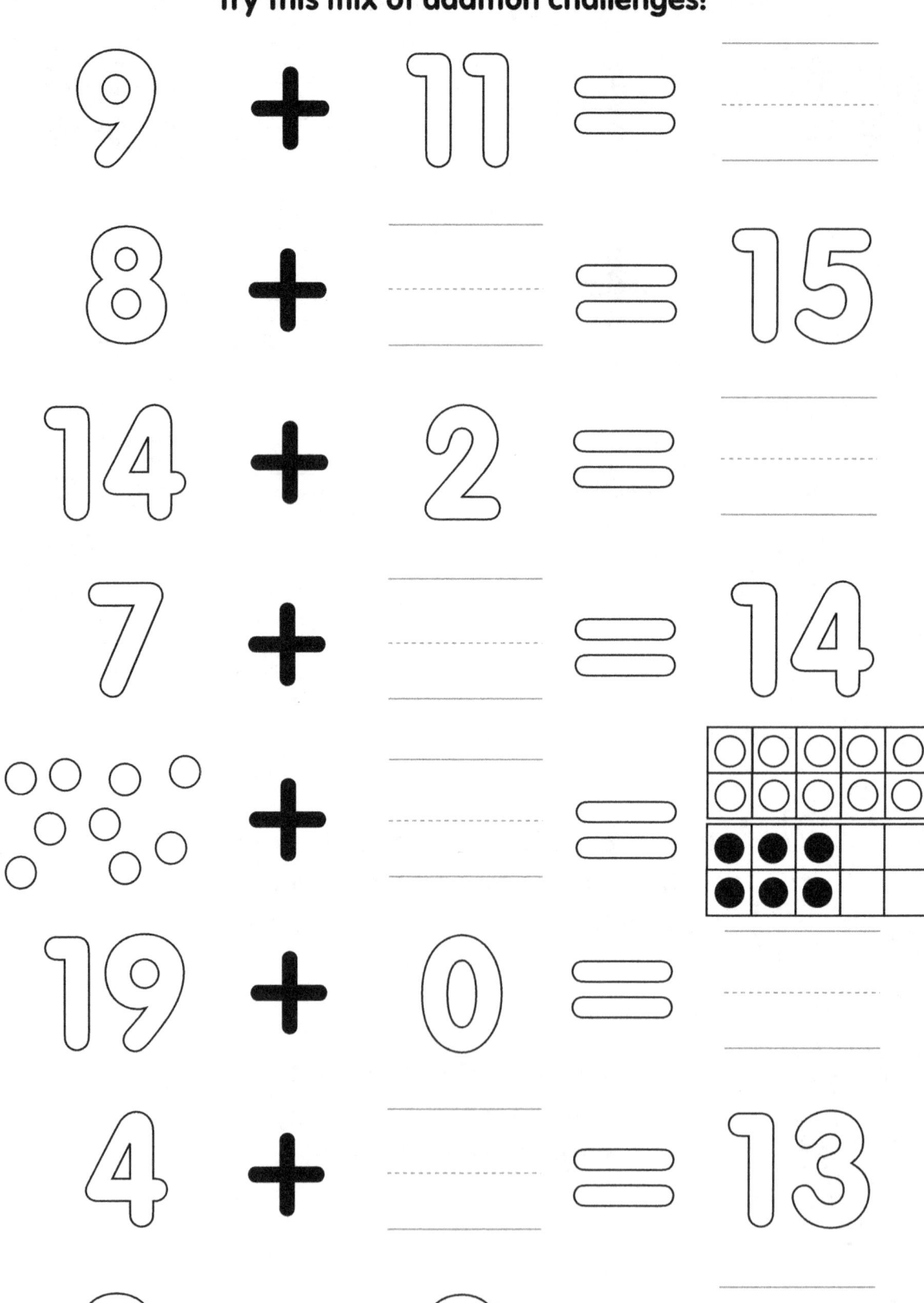

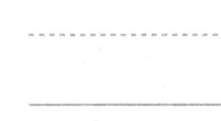

9 + 11 = _____

8 + _____ = 15

14 + 2 = _____

7 + _____ = 14

○○○○○○○○○○○○ + _____ = [ten frame: 10 empty + 6 filled]

19 + 0 = _____

4 + _____ = 13

8 + 8 = _____

Some of these additions are wrong! Draw around the CORRECT ones.

9 + 11 = 19

8 + 8 = 18

3 + 13 = 16

10 + 5 = 14

6 + 7 = 13

4 + ◯◯◯◯◯◯◯◯◯ = 9

◯◯◯◯◯ + 7 = 12

10 + ◯◯◯◯◯◯◯ = 17

◯◯◯◯◯◯◯ + △△△△△ = 13

16 + ◯◯◯◯ = 20

☆☆☆☆ + ☆☆☆ = 7

5 + ◯△◯△◯△◯☆ = 11

7 + 7 = 17

9 + ◯◯◯◯◯◯◯◯◯ = 18

3 + two = 6

six + ◯◯◯◯◯◯◯◯◯ = 15

11

Subtraction

Subtract the numbers or objects

Subtraction means the OPPOSITE of addition.

Addition means adding numbers to other numbers to make a BIGGER number.

Subtraction means taking numbers away from other numbers to make a SMALLER number.

For example, if you had 3 donuts and you gave 2 donuts to your friends, how many donuts would you have left?

Another way to say this is 3 − 2 =
DONUTS   SUBTRACT   DONUTS

We can use 10 FRAMES to help with subtraction too!
10 circles subtract 2 reveals the answer!

$10 - 2 = 8$

Use these 10 FRAMES to work out the answers.

① **Draw the number of dots in the first number.**

② **Cross out the number of dots in the second number.**

The first one is done for you.

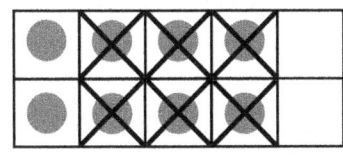

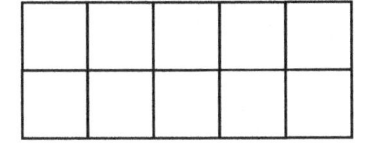

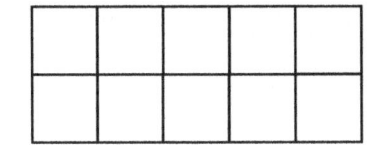

8 − 6 = 2

7 − 4 = ____

9 − 8 = ____

Now try with more 10 FRAMES for bigger subtractions!

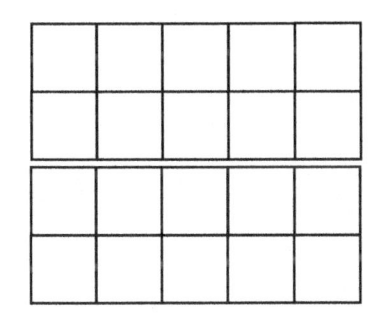

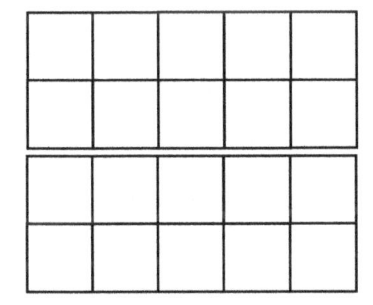

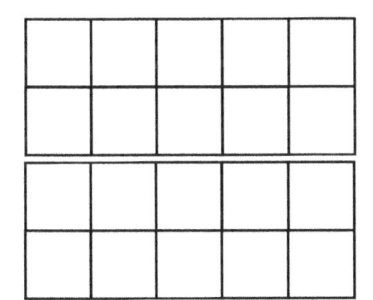

14 − 4 = ____

18 − 7 = ____

13 − 8 = ____

7 − 2 = _____

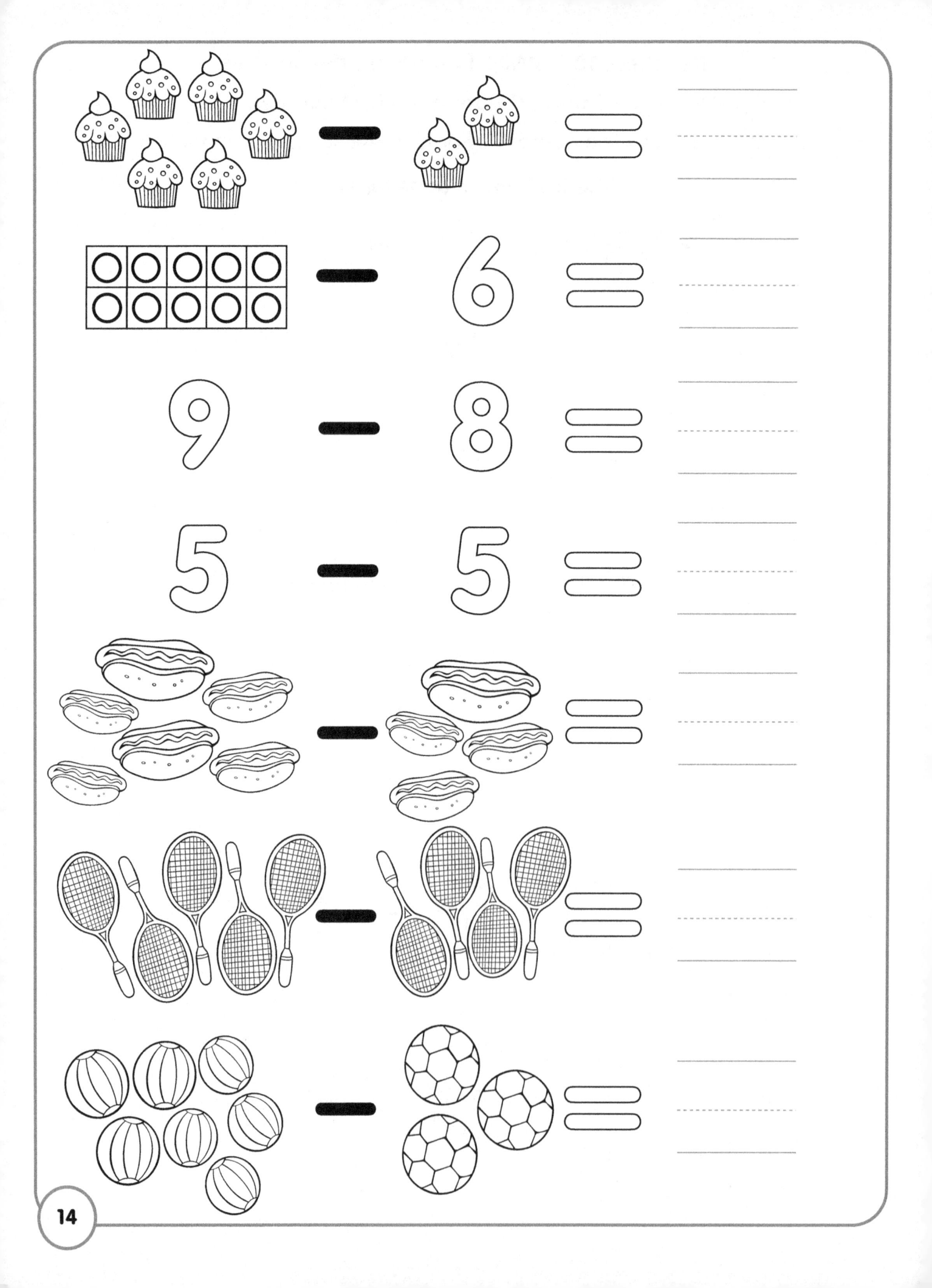

10 − 6 = _____

9 − 8 = _____

5 − 5 = _____

7 − 4 = _____

10 − 5 = _____

8 − 3 = _____

11 − 3 =

14 − 6 =

🌟 − 7 =

13 − 🎈 =

19 − 9 =

🦀 − 8 =

We can also change the sums we need to solve!

5 − _____ = 3

_____ − _____ = _____

If you had 6 scoops of ice cream and 2 melted in the sun, how many scoops would you have left?

There are 8 fish in a rockpool but 4 swim away. How many are left?

There are 10 friends on the bus. 6 friends get off at the bus stop. How many friends are left on the bus?

Some of these subtractions are wrong! Draw around the CORRECT ones.

11 − 3 = 9

8 − 8 = 1

14 − 4 = 10

20 − 5 = 5

8 − 6 = 2

11 − 9 = 2

7 − 2 = 4

13 − 7 = 6

9 − 4 = 4

18 − 4 = 14

13 − 5 = 5

13 − 5 = 9

7 − 7 = 0

17 − 13 = 2

18 − two = 16

ten − 8 = 8

Color by Numbers

Each area to color has an addition or subtraction in it.
Work out the answer, then see what color to use!

ANSWER =	3	4	5	6	7
COLOR =	RED	BLUE	YELLOW	GREEN	BLACK

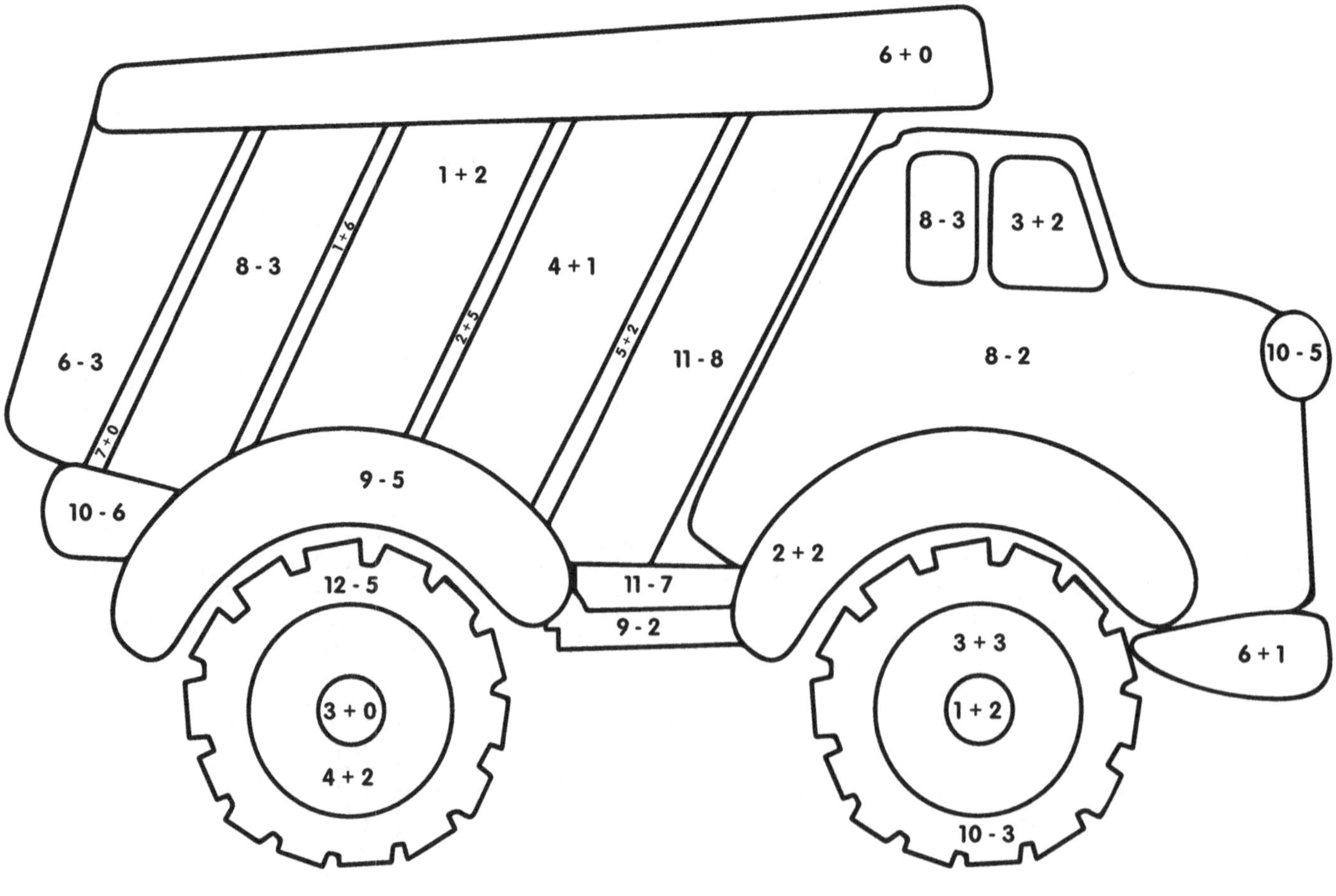
6 + 0
1 + 2
8 - 3
1+6
4 + 1
6 - 3
2+5
5+2
11 - 8
8 - 3
3 + 2
8 - 2
10 - 5
7+0
9 - 5
10 - 6
2 + 2
12 - 5
11 - 7
9 - 2
3 + 3
6 + 1
3 + 0
1 + 2
4 + 2
10 - 3

Color by Numbers

Each area to color has an addition or subtraction in it. Work out the answer, then see what color to use!

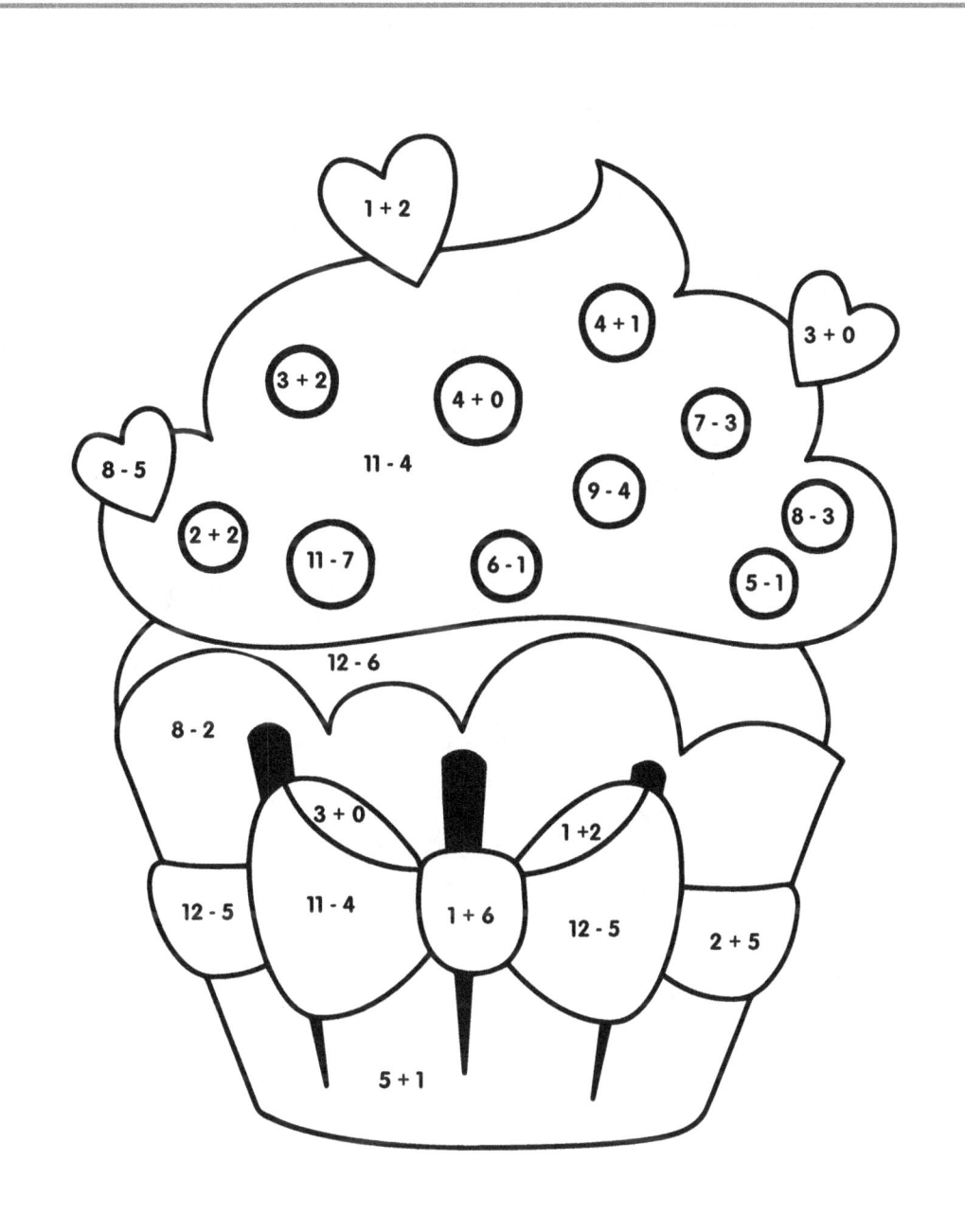

ANSWER =	3	4	5	6	7
COLOR =	RED	BLUE	YELLOW	GREEN	PINK

1 + 2
4 + 1
3 + 0
3 + 2
4 + 0
7 - 3
8 - 5
11 - 4
9 - 4
8 - 3
2 + 2
11 - 7
6 - 1
5 - 1
12 - 6
8 - 2
3 + 0
1 + 2
12 - 5
11 - 4
1 + 6
12 - 5
2 + 5
5 + 1

19

Make your own MATH flash cards!

Color-in and cut-out the double-sided cards from the following pages to make your own unique number flash cards for fun challenges!

① **Color-in both sides of the cards in any color you like!**

COLOR IN THE RIGHT NUMBER OF DOTS FOR EACH CARD

COLOR IN THE RIGHT NUMBER OF DOTS FOR EACH CARD

② **Cut the cards out by cutting along the dotted lines.** Be careful with the scissors!

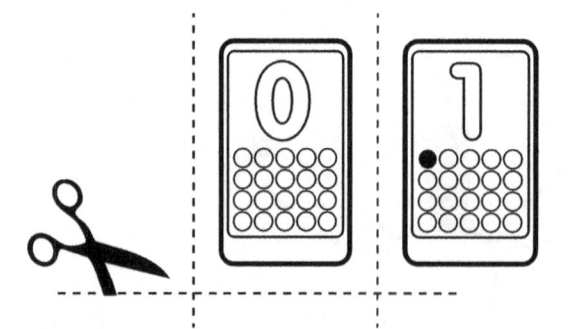

③ **Make your own number challenges. MIX 'N' MATCH easy or hard!**

0	1	2
3	4	5
6	7	8

TWO	ONE	ZERO
FIVE	FOUR	THREE
EIGHT	SEVEN	SIX

9 10 11

12 13 14

15 16 17

ELEVEN	TEN	NINE
FOURTEEN	THIRTEEN	TWELVE
SEVENTEEN	SIXTEEN	FIFTEEN

18	19	20
?	−	+
=	−	+

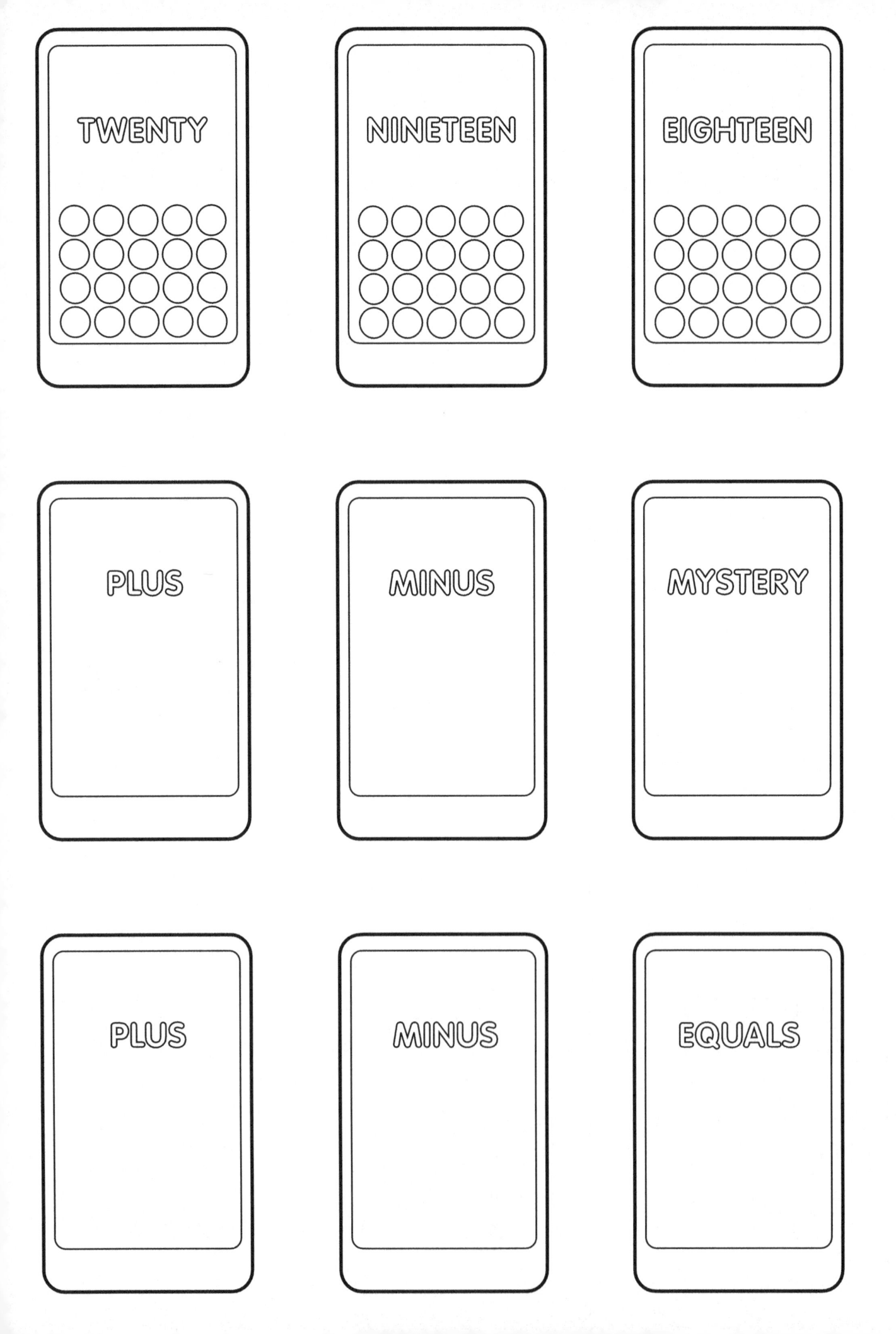

TWENTY	NINETEEN	EIGHTEEN
PLUS	MINUS	MYSTERY
PLUS	MINUS	EQUALS

Number Connect

The same number can be shown in lots of different ways

For example, all of these show the same number.

3   ○○○   three

Draw a line to connect the same numbers together.

1
6
8
4
7
2

four
eight
seven
six
two
one

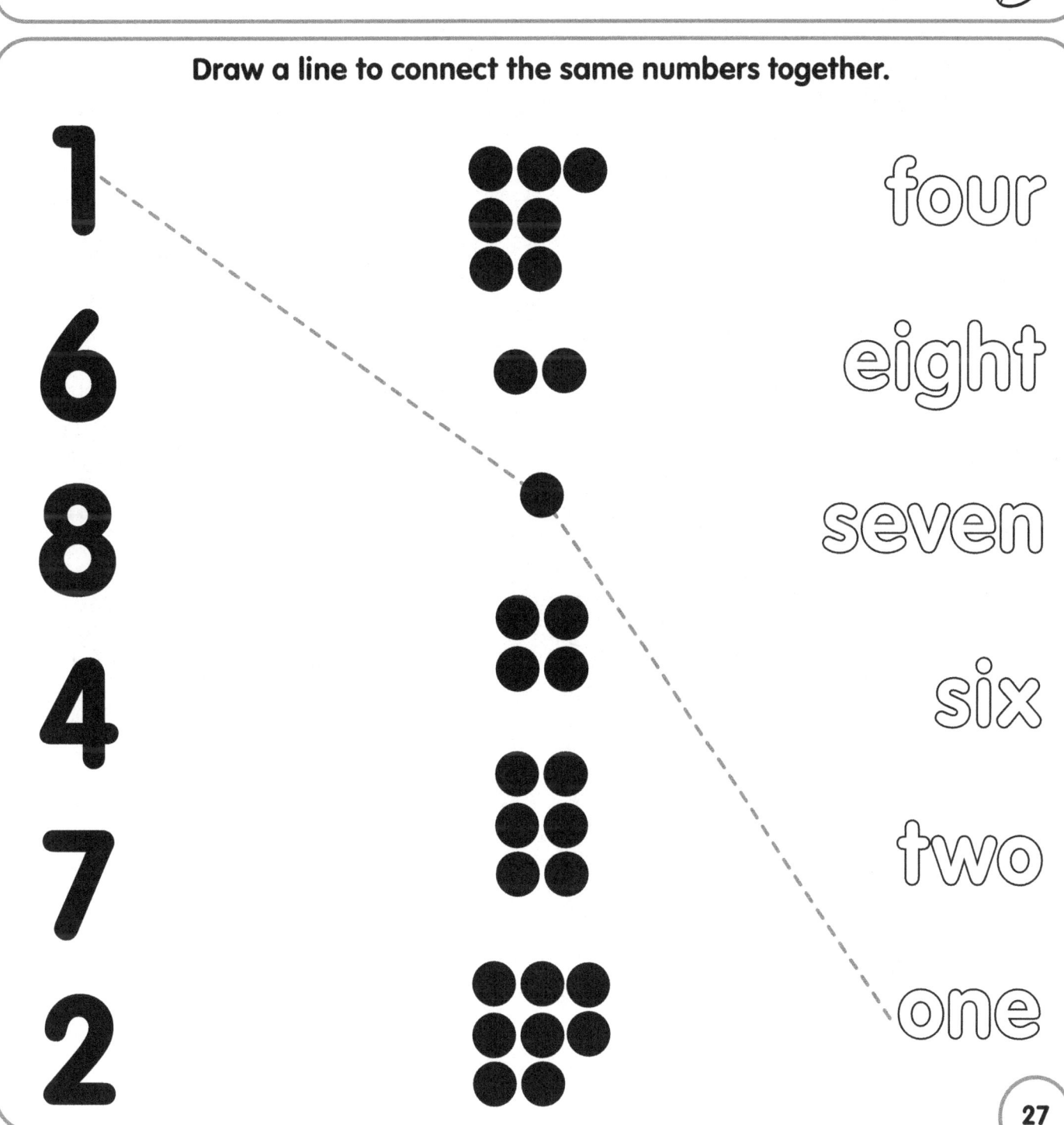

What a mess!
Can you draw lines to connect all the same numbers together?

8   1

two   2   five

one

eight   5   four

4

28

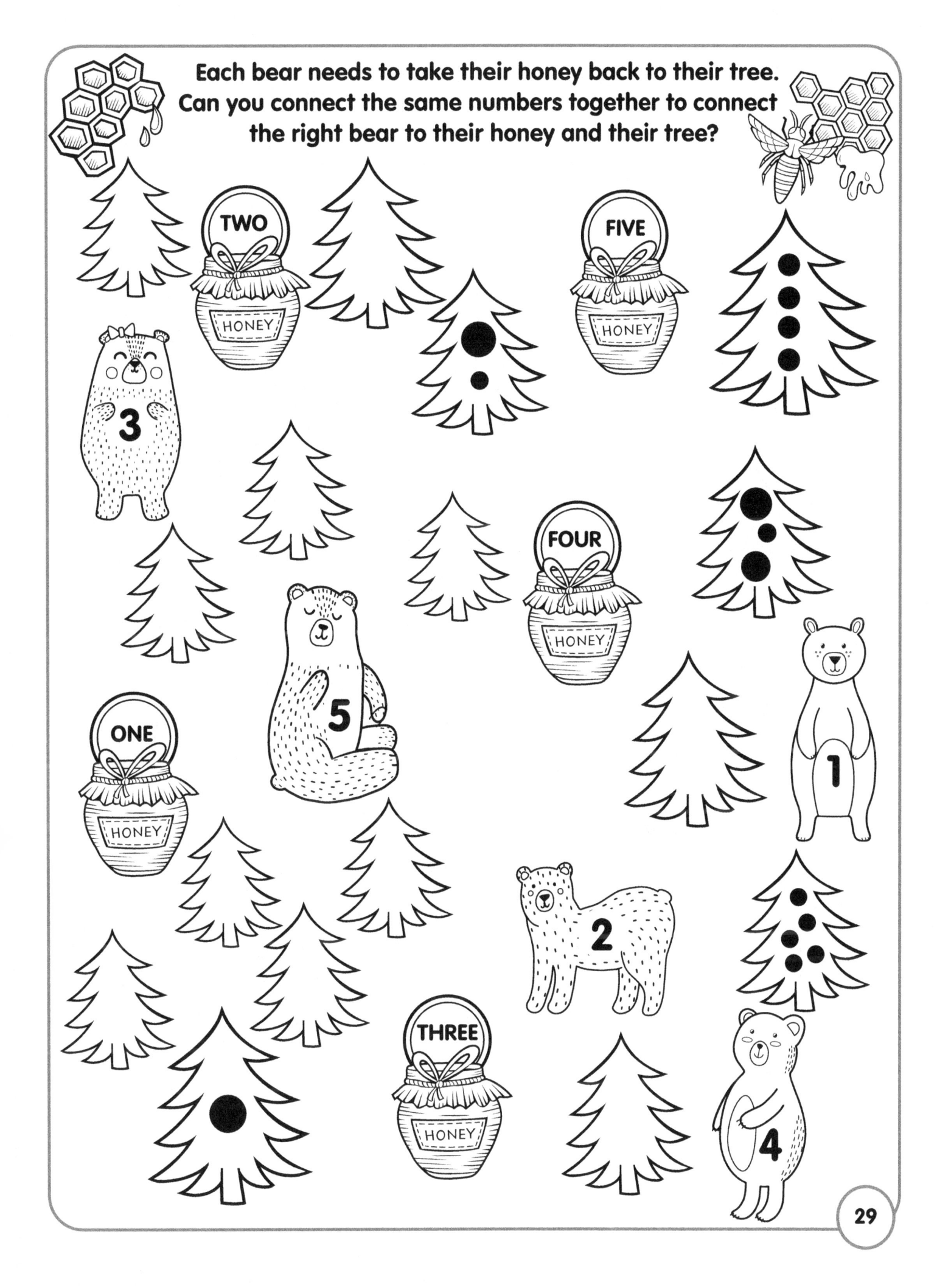

Each bear needs to take their honey back to their tree. Can you connect the same numbers together to connect the right bear to their honey and their tree?

We're going on holiday! Can you help fly the plane to the beach?
Color a number path in the correct order from 1 to 20 to reach the beach.

REMEMBER The same number can be shown in different ways!

Number Lines

Number lines can help to visualize, count and compare numbers easily

Number lines can connect any 2 numbers for example:

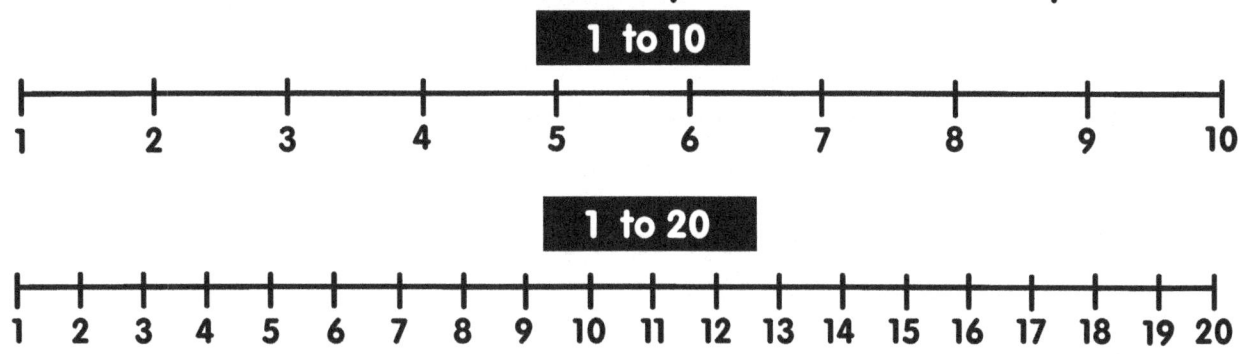

1 to 10

1 2 3 4 5 6 7 8 9 10

1 to 20

1 2 3 4 5 6 7 8 9 10 11 12 13 14 15 16 17 18 19 20

A rabbit is sitting at number 2 and hops forwards 3 numbers. What number does she get to?

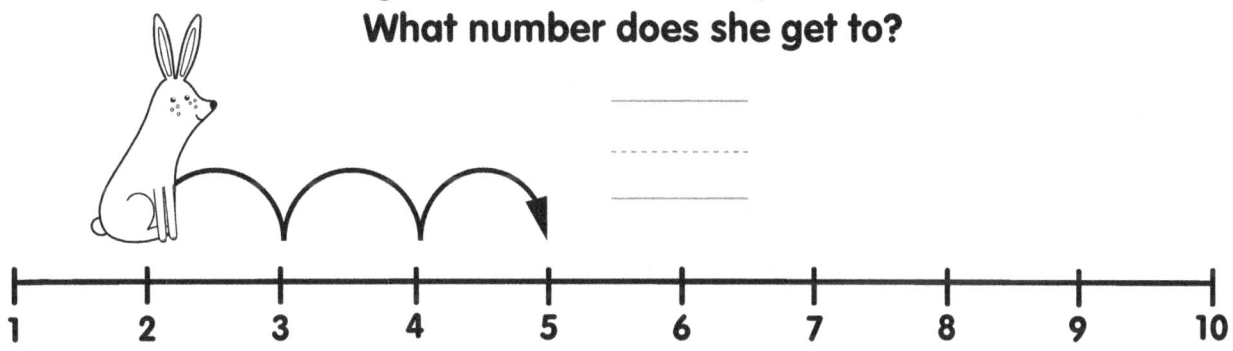

1 2 3 4 5 6 7 8 9 10

Another rabbit starts at number 1 and hops forwards 5 numbers. Draw his 5 hops.

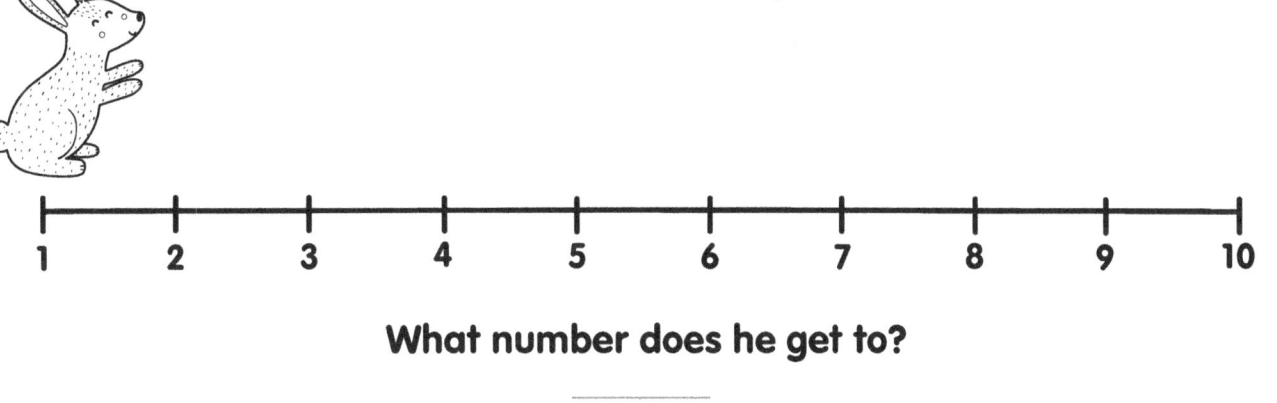

1 2 3 4 5 6 7 8 9 10

What number does he get to?

31

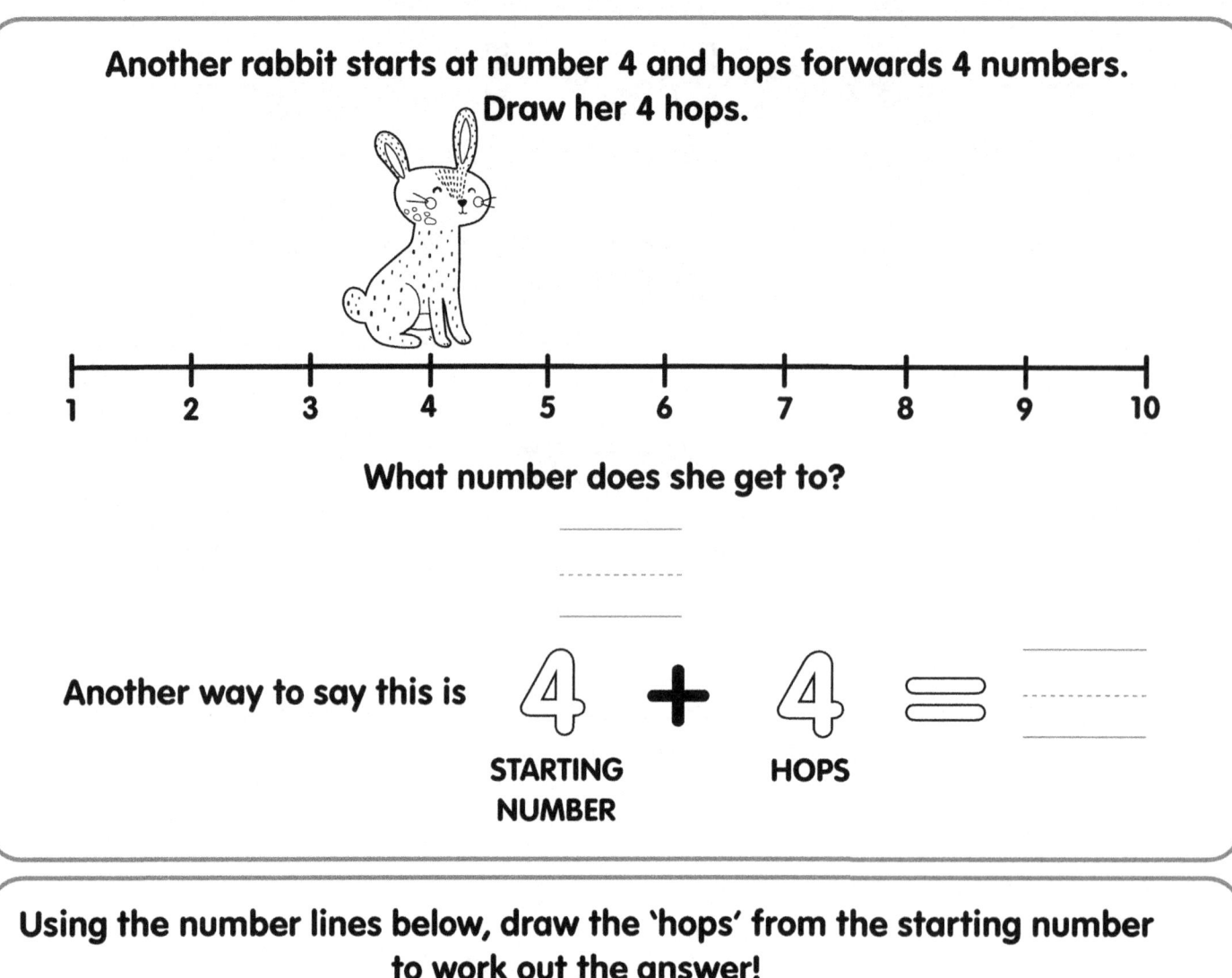

Another rabbit starts at number 4 and hops forwards 4 numbers. Draw her 4 hops.

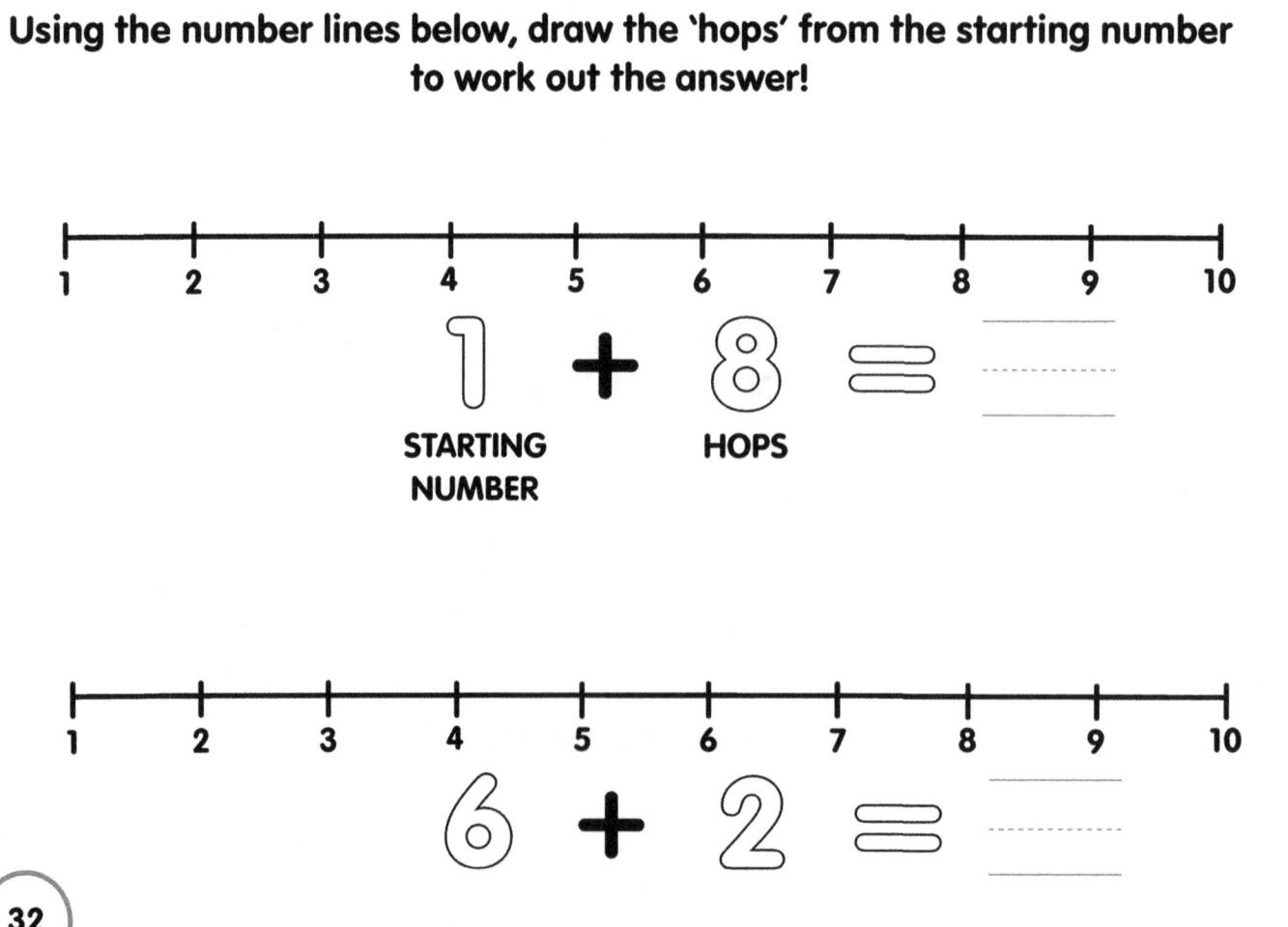

1 2 3 4 5 6 7 8 9 10

What number does she get to?

_____

Another way to say this is 4 + 4 = _____

STARTING NUMBER   HOPS

Using the number lines below, draw the 'hops' from the starting number to work out the answer!

1 2 3 4 5 6 7 8 9 10

1 + 8 = _____

STARTING NUMBER   HOPS

1 2 3 4 5 6 7 8 9 10

6 + 2 = _____

32

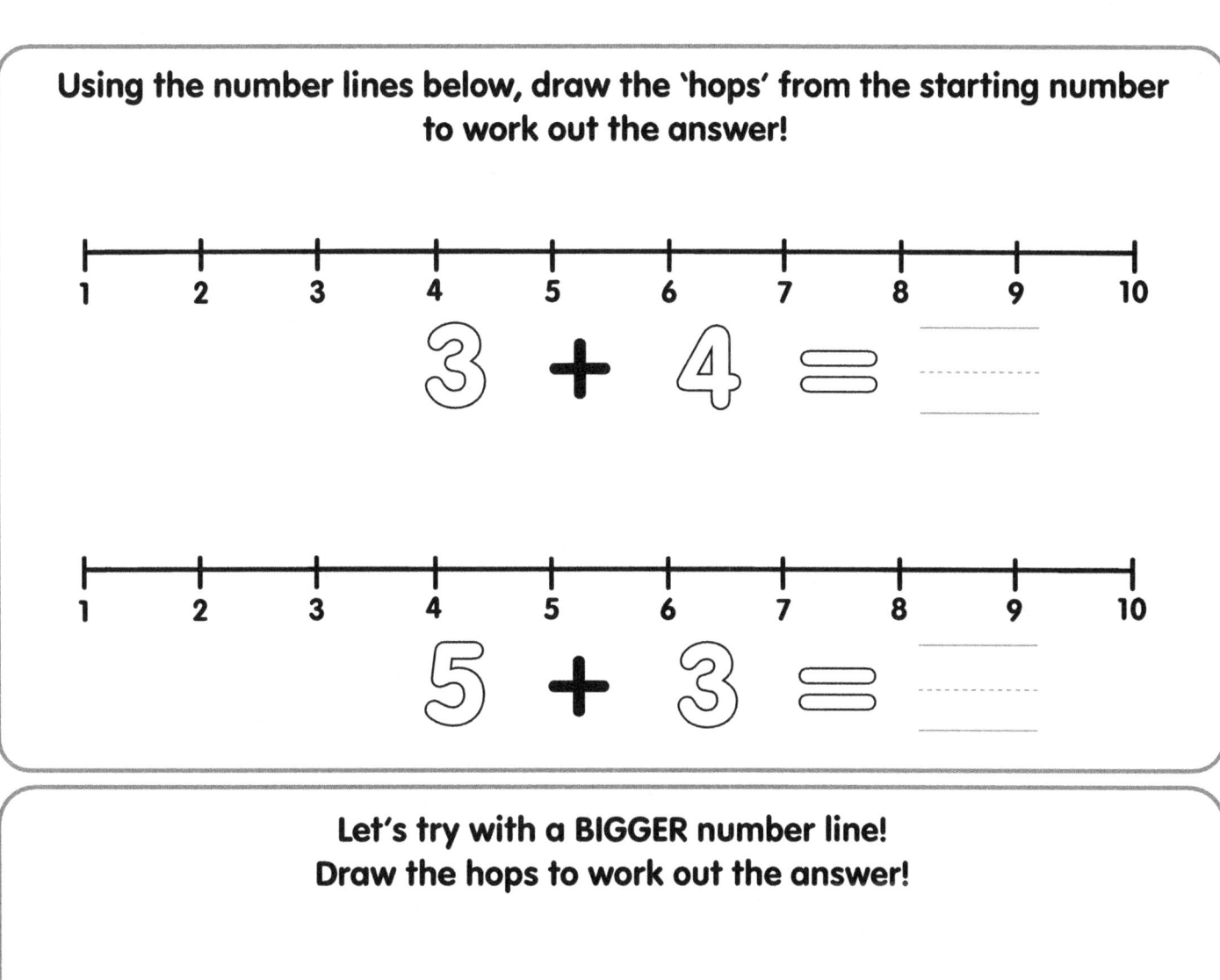

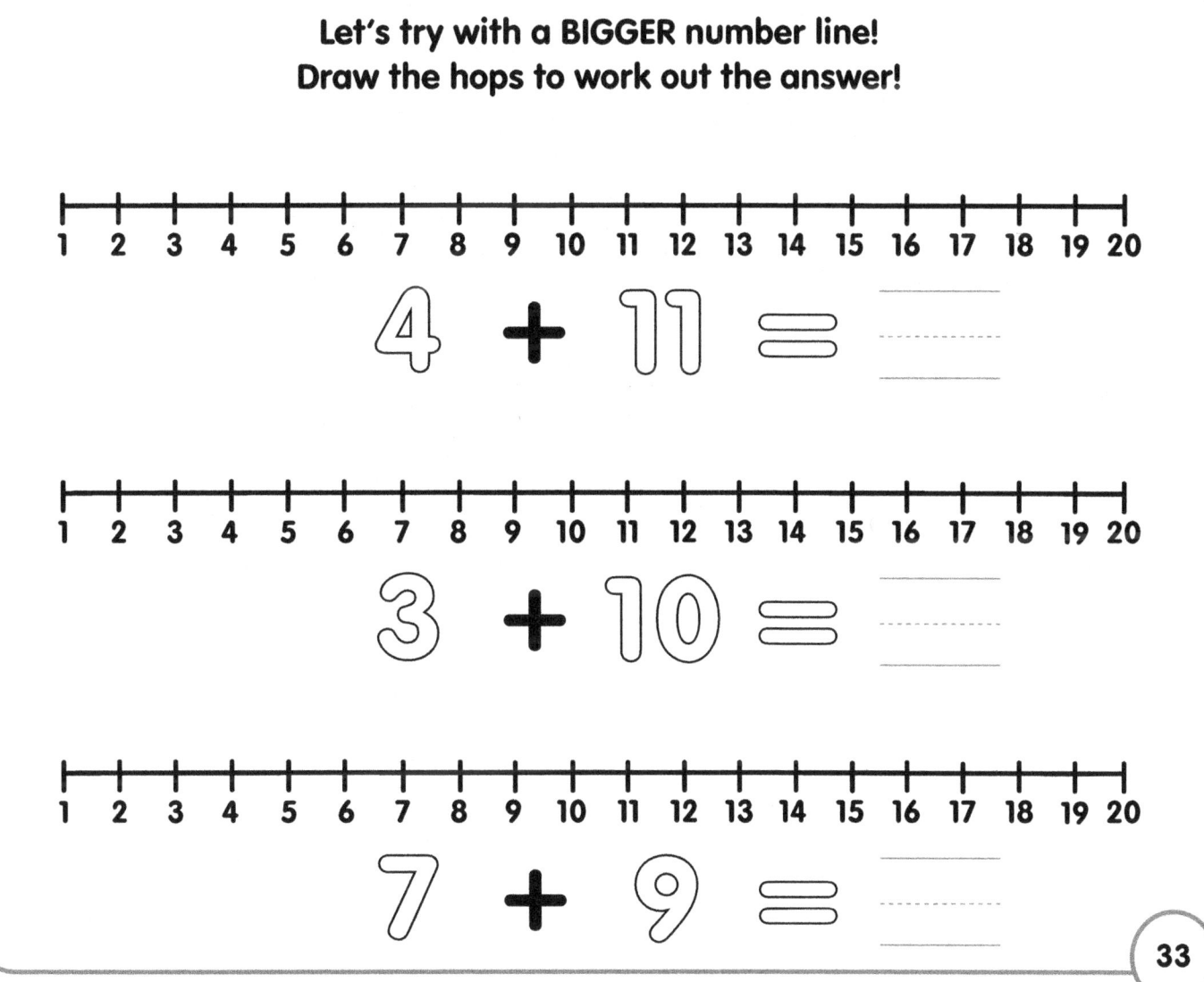

Using the number lines below, draw the 'hops' from the starting number to work out the answer!

1 2 3 4 5 6 7 8 9 10

3 + 4 = ____

1 2 3 4 5 6 7 8 9 10

5 + 3 = ____

Let's try with a BIGGER number line! Draw the hops to work out the answer!

1 2 3 4 5 6 7 8 9 10 11 12 13 14 15 16 17 18 19 20

4 + 11 = ____

1 2 3 4 5 6 7 8 9 10 11 12 13 14 15 16 17 18 19 20

3 + 10 = ____

1 2 3 4 5 6 7 8 9 10 11 12 13 14 15 16 17 18 19 20

7 + 9 = ____

Number lines can help with subtraction too!
A rabbit is sitting at number 9 and hops back 6 numbers.
What number does he get to?

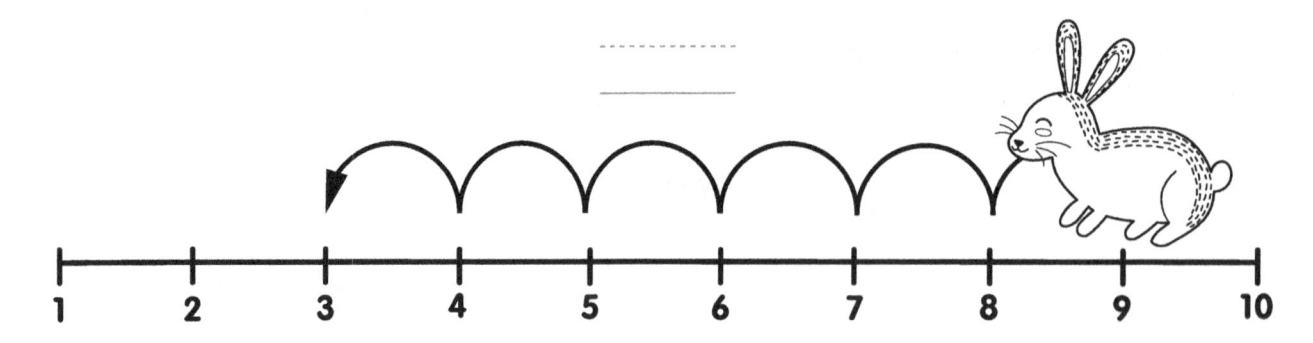

Another rabbit starts at number 5 and hops back 3 numbers.
Draw her 3 hops.

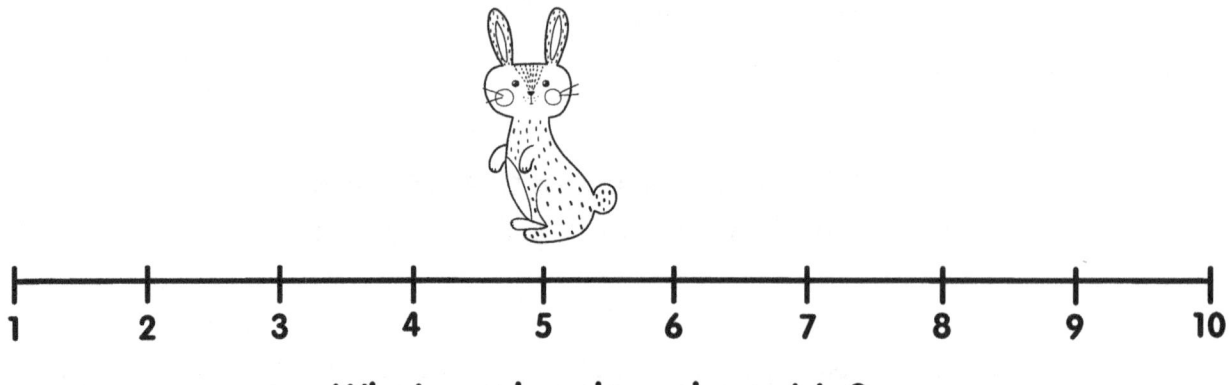

What number does she get to?

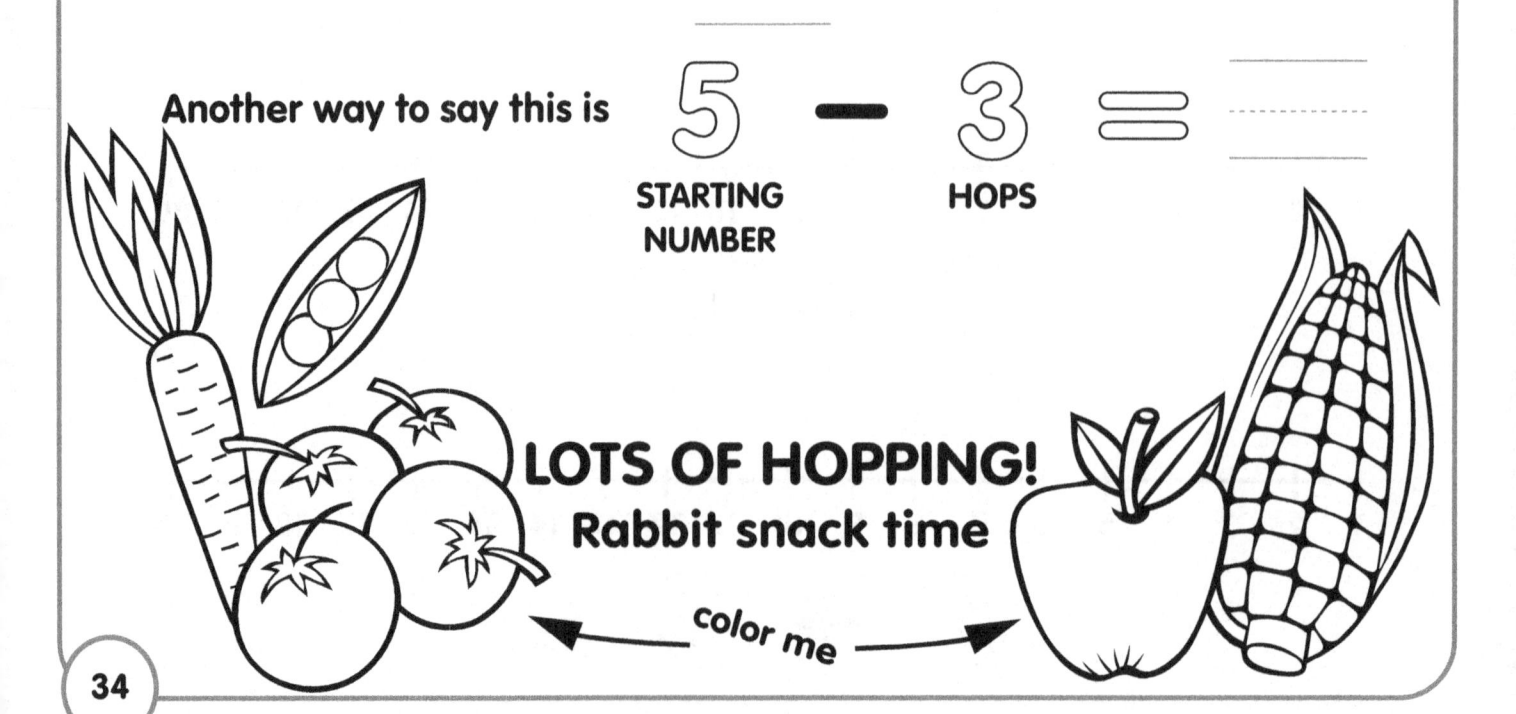

Another way to say this is   5   −   3   =
                    STARTING   HOPS
                    NUMBER

LOTS OF HOPPING!
Rabbit snack time

color me

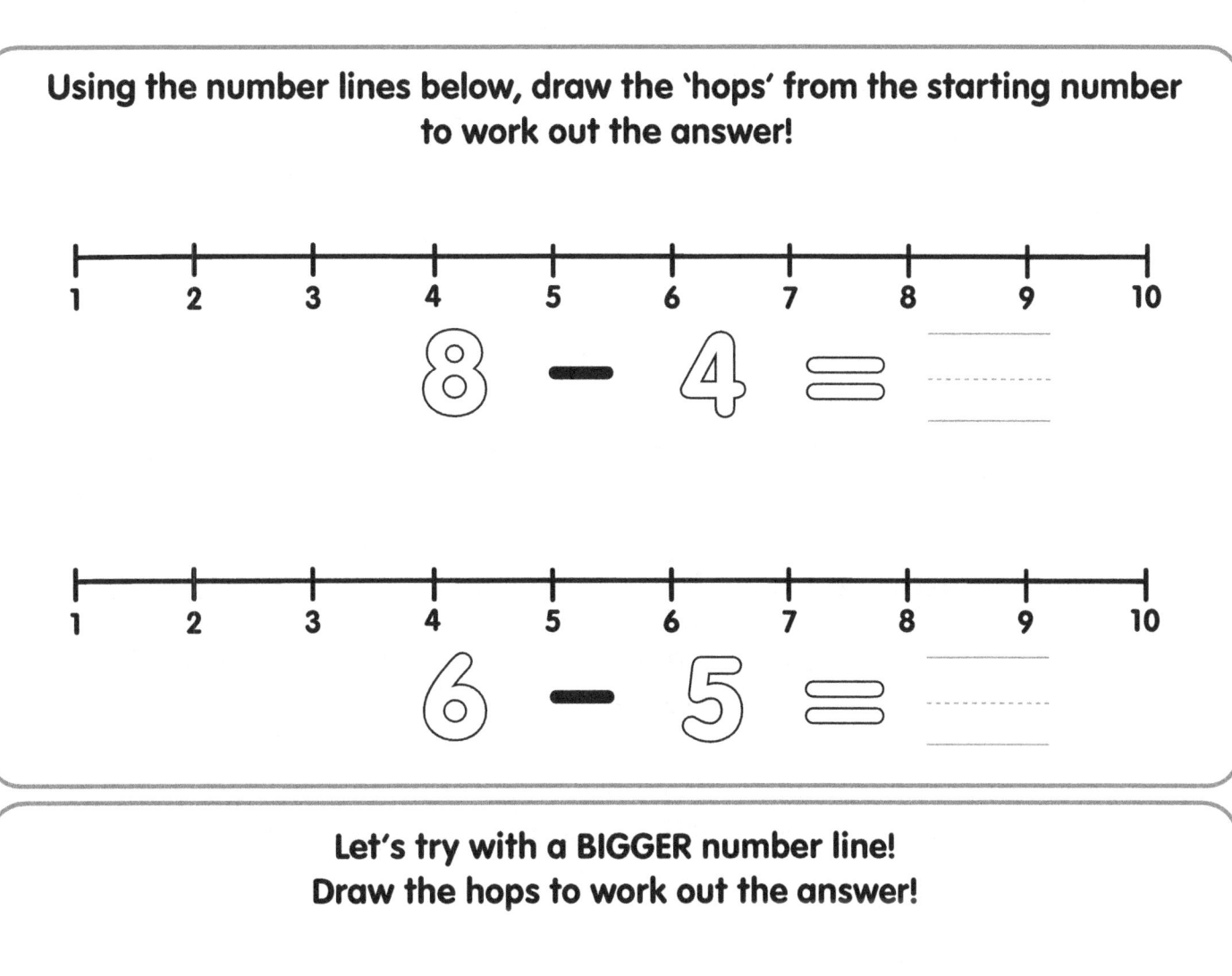

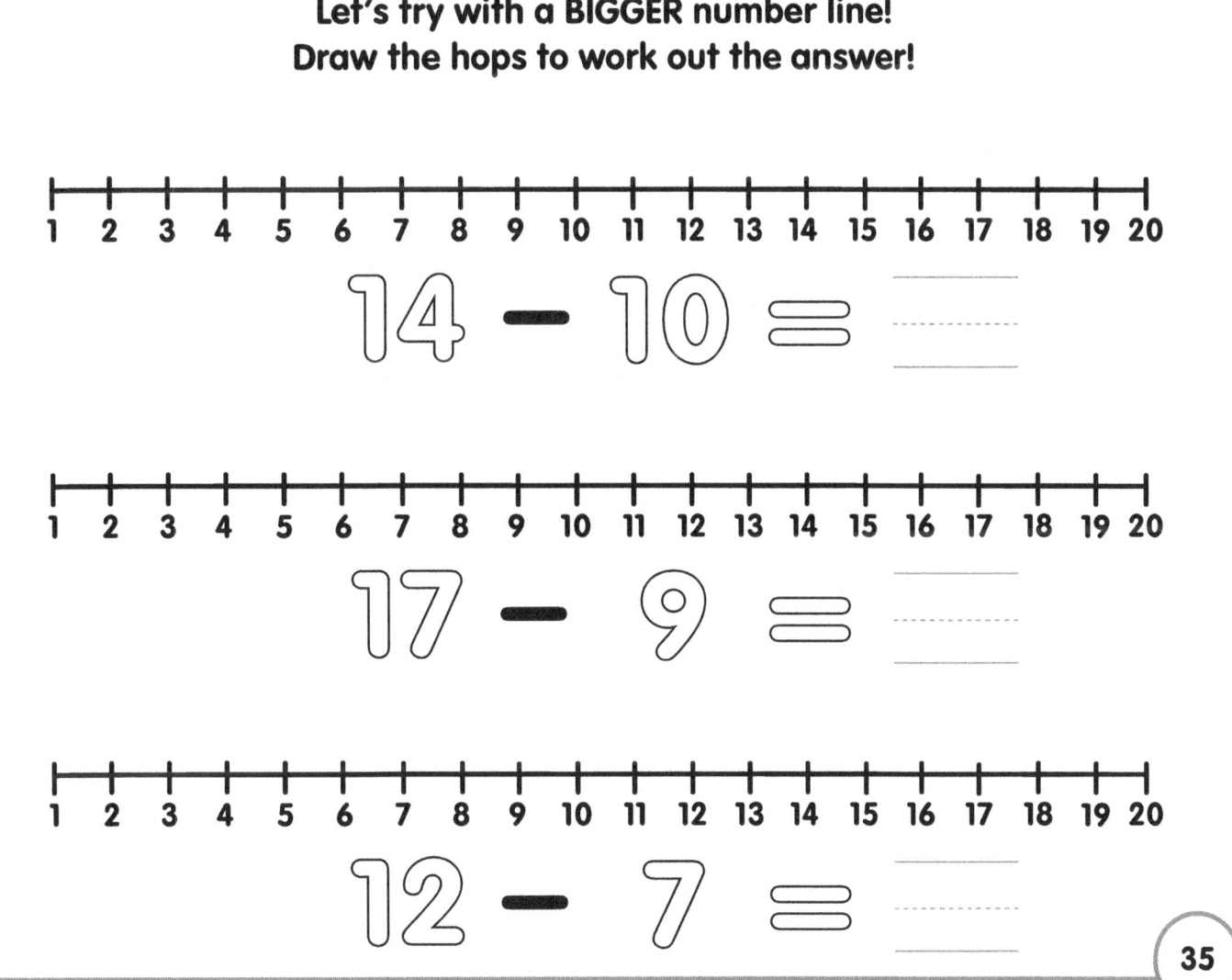

Using the number lines below, draw the 'hops' from the starting number to work out the answer!

|—+—+—+—+—+—+—+—+—|
1 2 3 4 5 6 7 8 9 10

8 − 4 =

|—+—+—+—+—+—+—+—+—|
1 2 3 4 5 6 7 8 9 10

6 − 5 =

Let's try with a BIGGER number line! Draw the hops to work out the answer!

|—+—+—+—+—+—+—+—+—+—+—+—+—+—+—+—+—+—+—|
1 2 3 4 5 6 7 8 9 10 11 12 13 14 15 16 17 18 19 20

14 − 10 =

|—+—+—+—+—+—+—+—+—+—+—+—+—+—+—+—+—+—+—|
1 2 3 4 5 6 7 8 9 10 11 12 13 14 15 16 17 18 19 20

17 − 9 =

|—+—+—+—+—+—+—+—+—+—+—+—+—+—+—+—+—+—+—|
1 2 3 4 5 6 7 8 9 10 11 12 13 14 15 16 17 18 19 20

12 − 7 =

We can use number lines to help our rabbits get to their lunch!
A hungry rabbit is sitting at number 2 but his carrot is at number 9.
How many hops does he need to do to get to the carrot?

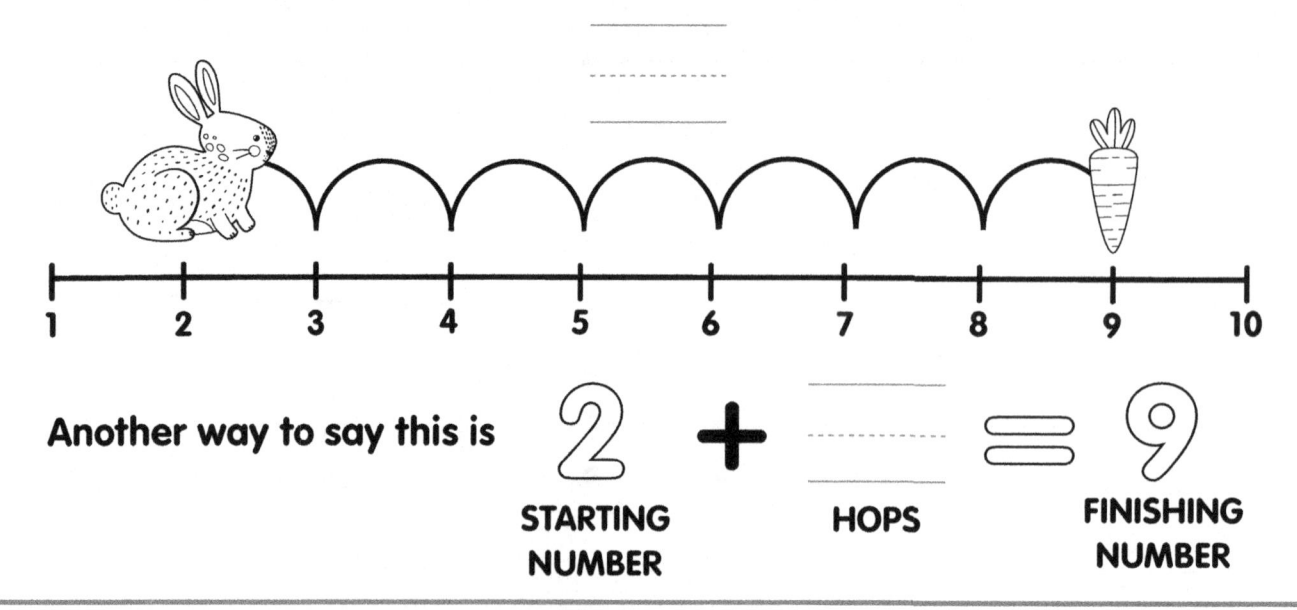

1 2 3 4 5 6 7 8 9 10

Another way to say this is 2 + ___ = 9
STARTING NUMBER   HOPS   FINISHING NUMBER

Using the number lines below, draw the 'hops' from the starting number to the finishing number to work out the answer!

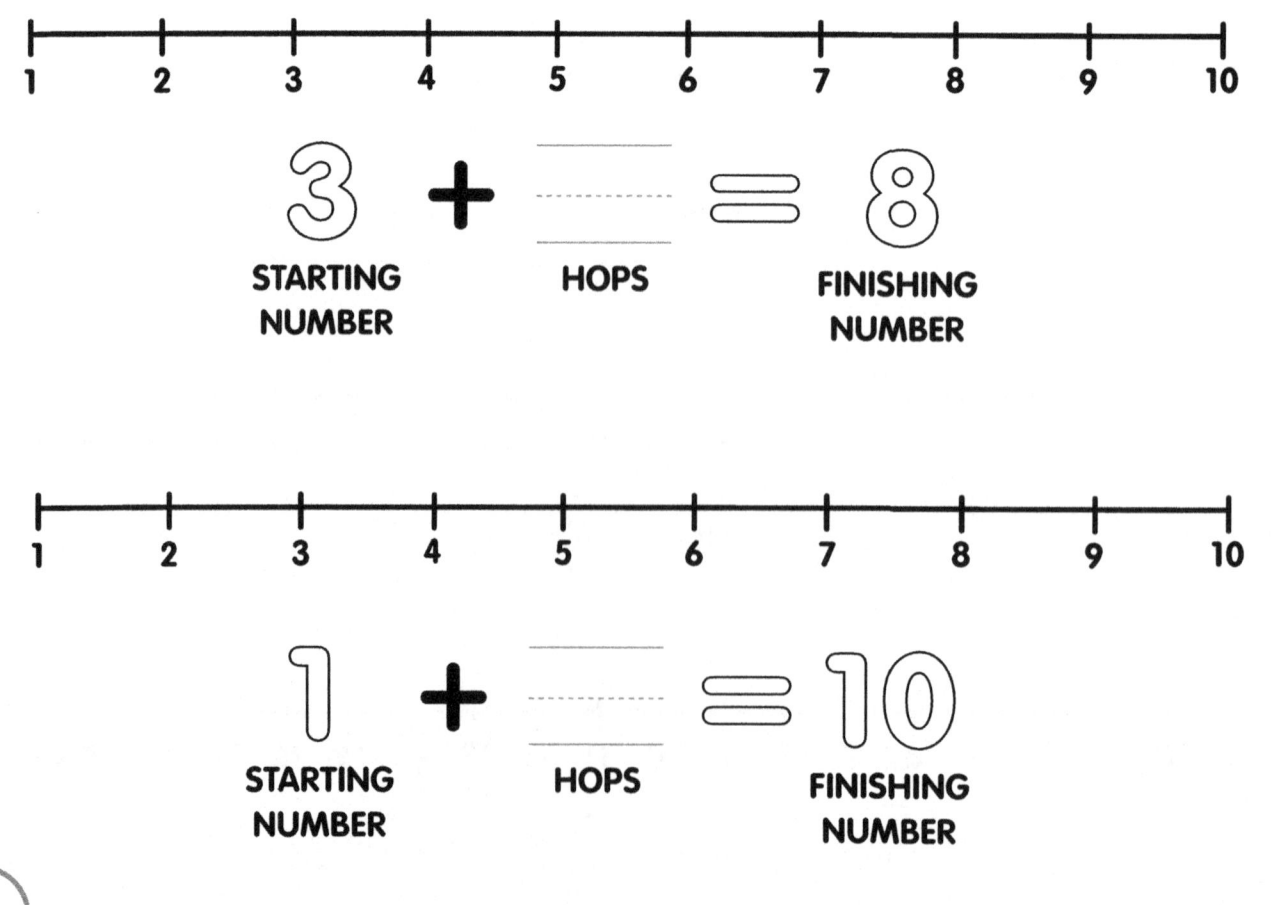

1 2 3 4 5 6 7 8 9 10

3 + ___ = 8
STARTING NUMBER   HOPS   FINISHING NUMBER

1 2 3 4 5 6 7 8 9 10

1 + ___ = 10
STARTING NUMBER   HOPS   FINISHING NUMBER

36

**Let's try with a BIGGER number line!
Draw the hops to work out the answer!**

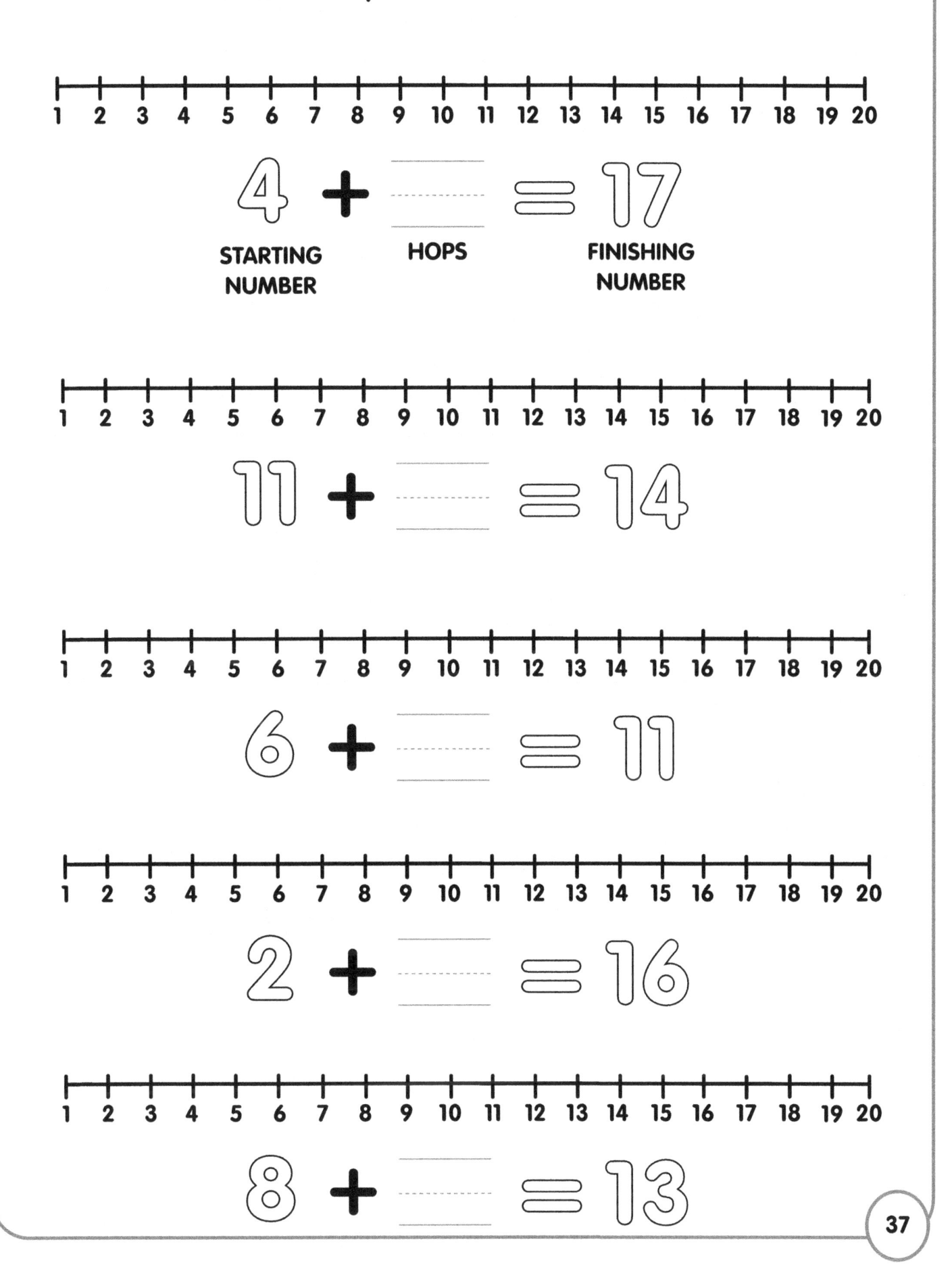

1 2 3 4 5 6 7 8 9 10 11 12 13 14 15 16 17 18 19 20

4 + ___ = 17

STARTING NUMBER HOPS FINISHING NUMBER

1 2 3 4 5 6 7 8 9 10 11 12 13 14 15 16 17 18 19 20

11 + ___ = 14

1 2 3 4 5 6 7 8 9 10 11 12 13 14 15 16 17 18 19 20

6 + ___ = 11

1 2 3 4 5 6 7 8 9 10 11 12 13 14 15 16 17 18 19 20

2 + ___ = 16

1 2 3 4 5 6 7 8 9 10 11 12 13 14 15 16 17 18 19 20

8 + ___ = 13

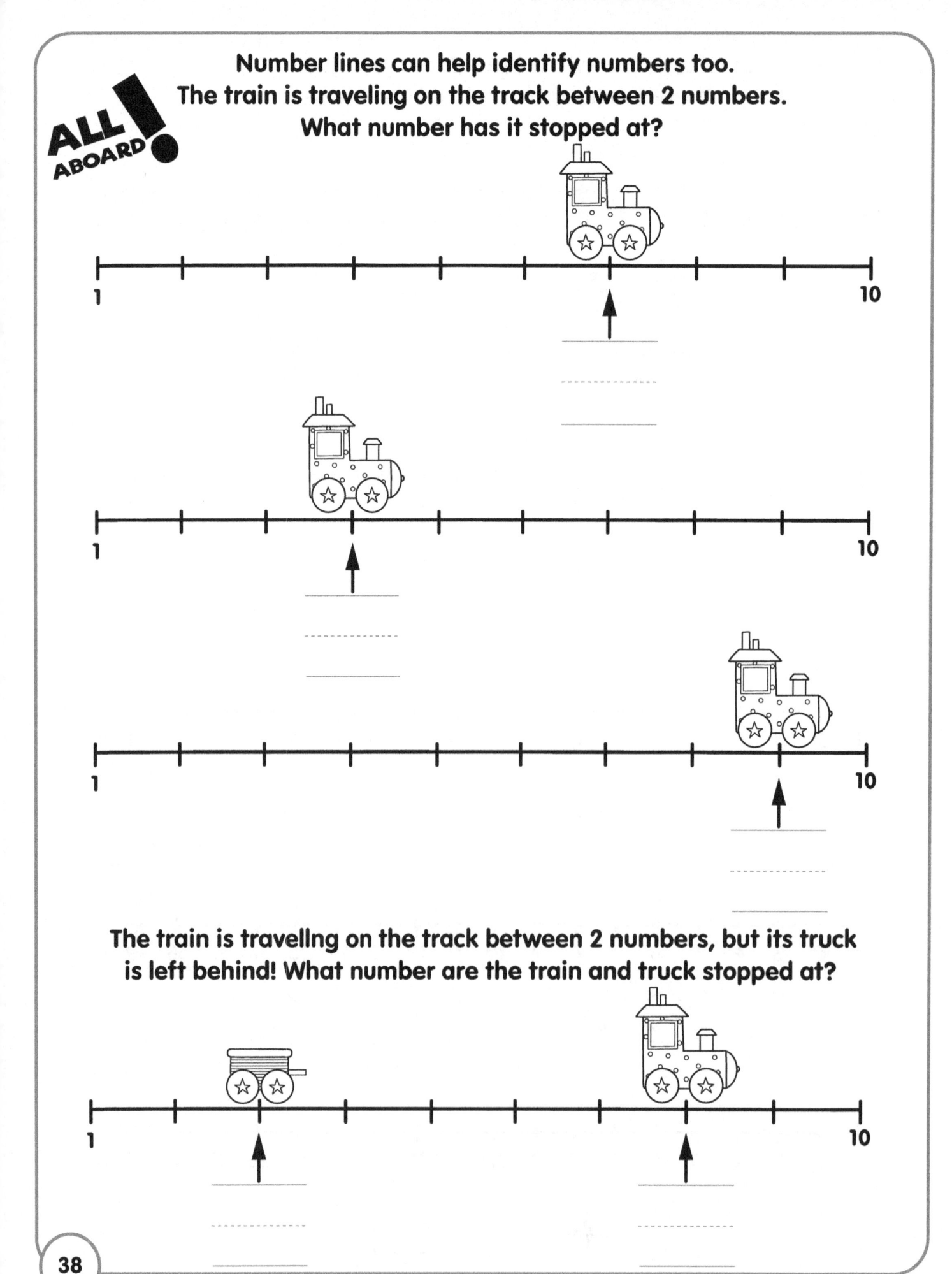

**Number lines can help identify numbers too.
The train is traveling on the track between 2 numbers.
What number has it stopped at?**

The train is travelling on the track between 2 numbers, but its truck is left behind! What number are the train and truck stopped at?

38

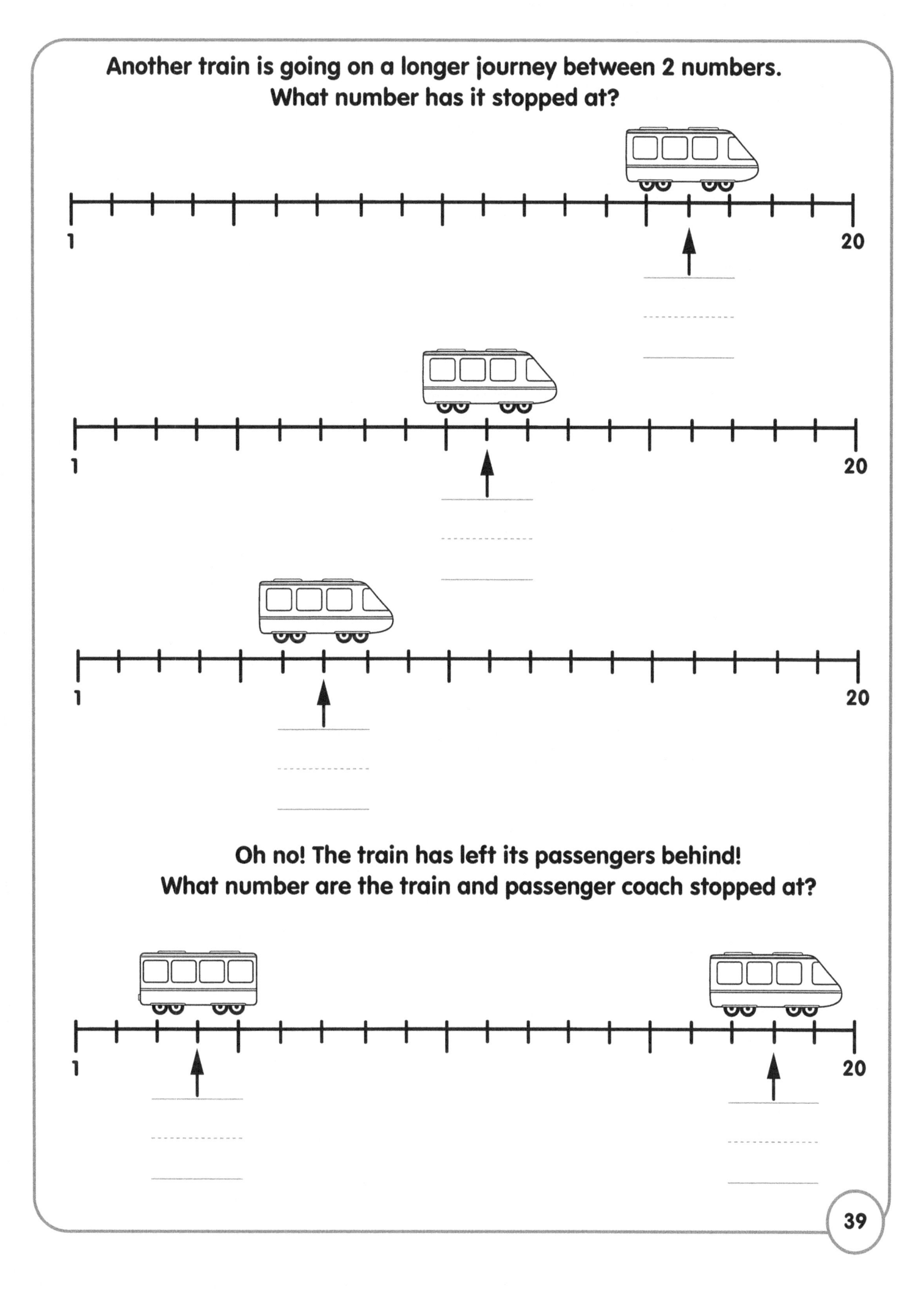

**Another train is going on a longer journey between 2 numbers.
What number has it stopped at?**

**Oh no! The train has left its passengers behind!
What number are the train and passenger coach stopped at?**

Using all your Super Star skills from hopping rabbits and speedy trains, can you find the answers to these questions?

Write down the missing 2 numbers to get the right answer!

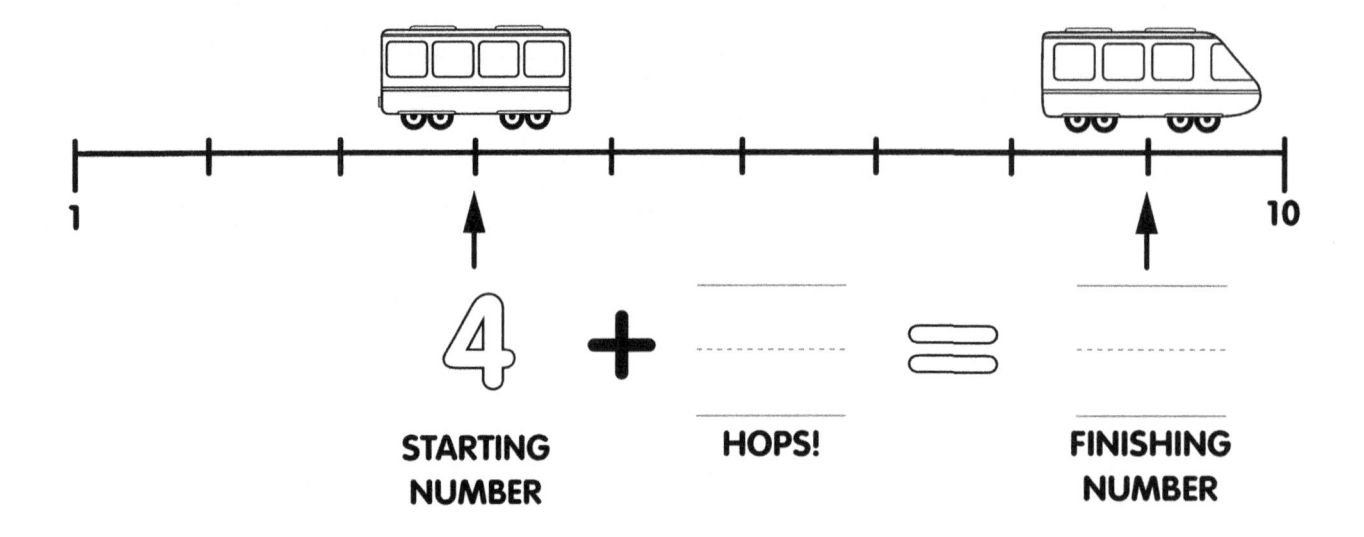

4 + ___ = ___

STARTING NUMBER   HOPS!   FINISHING NUMBER

Write down the missing 2 numbers to get the right answer!

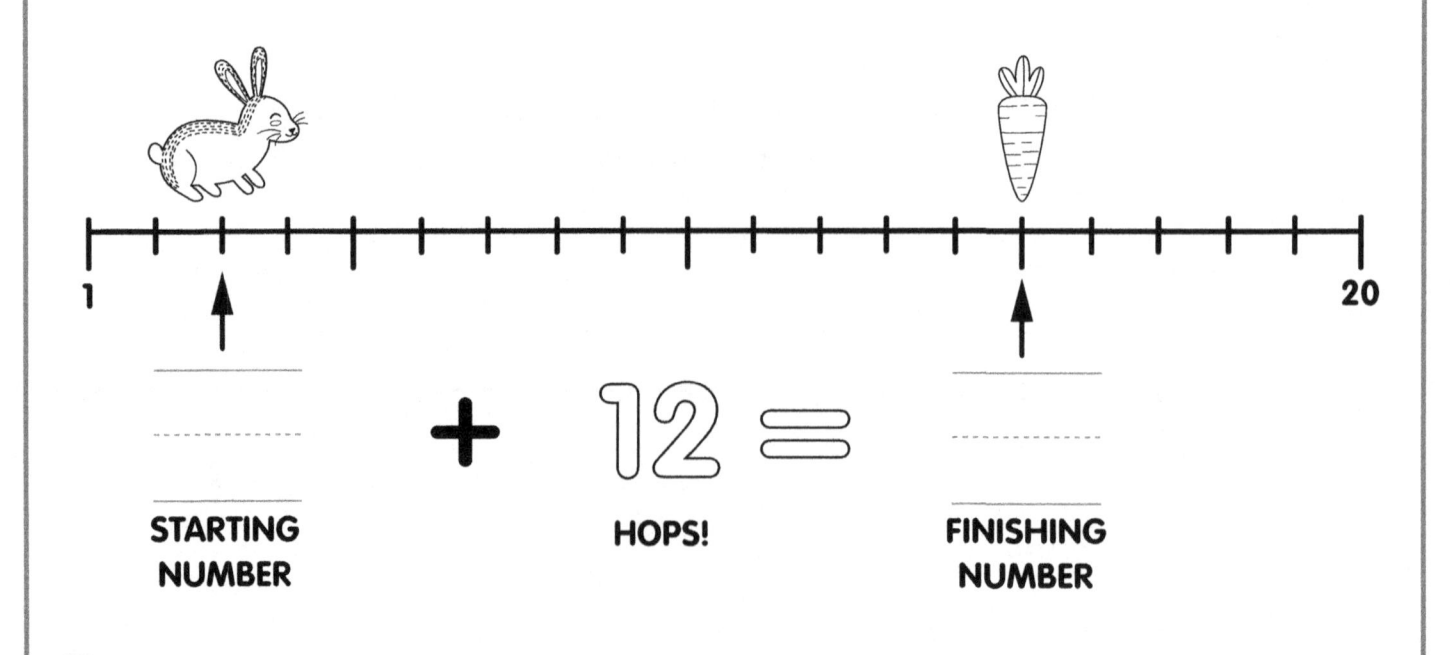

___ + 12 = ___

STARTING NUMBER   HOPS!   FINISHING NUMBER

Skip Counting

As well as counting in 1s, we can skip numbers and count in any number we like!

A rabbit is sitting at number 2 and can hop 2 numbers at a time. What number does she get to?

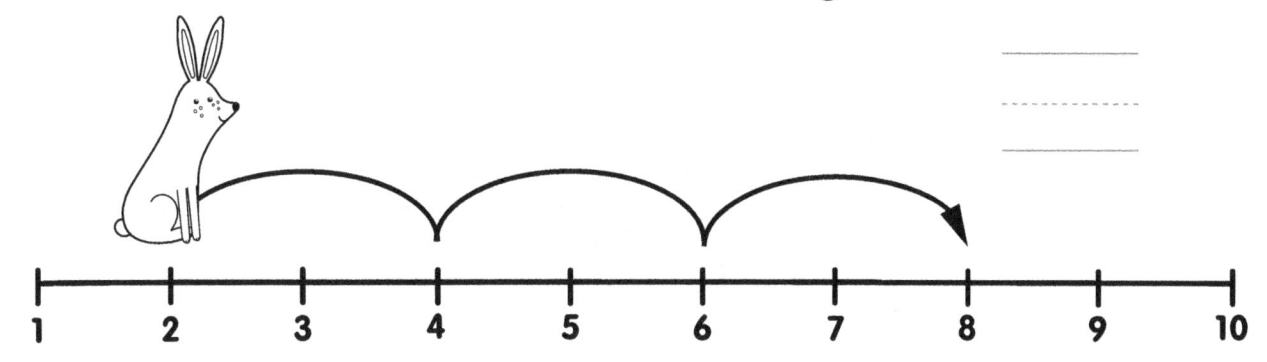

A rabbit is sitting at number 3 and can hop 3 numbers at a time. What number does he get to?

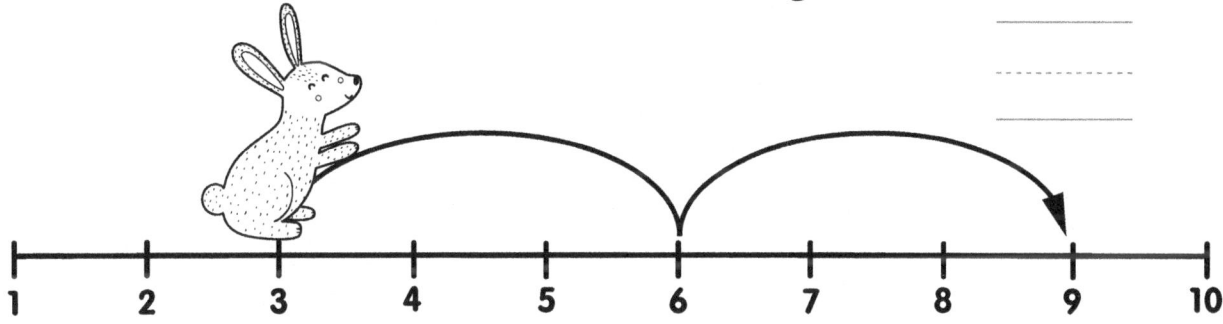

You can skip count using any number.
For example, to count in 5's you ADD 5 to a number each time.

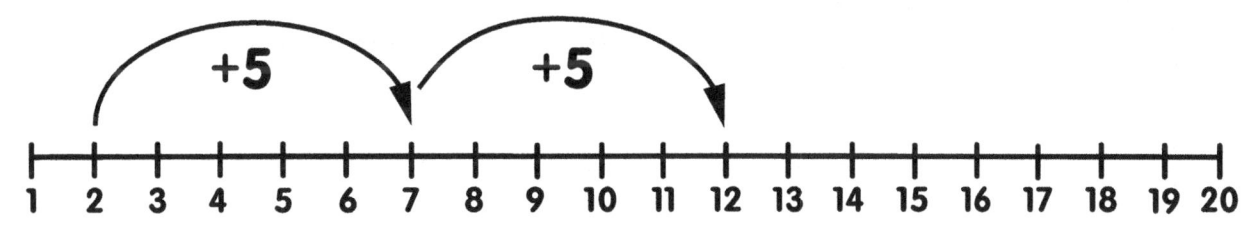

What would be the next number after 12 if you were counting in 5's?

Draw the hops for the rabbit, counting in 2's, all the way to 20.
The first hop is done for you.

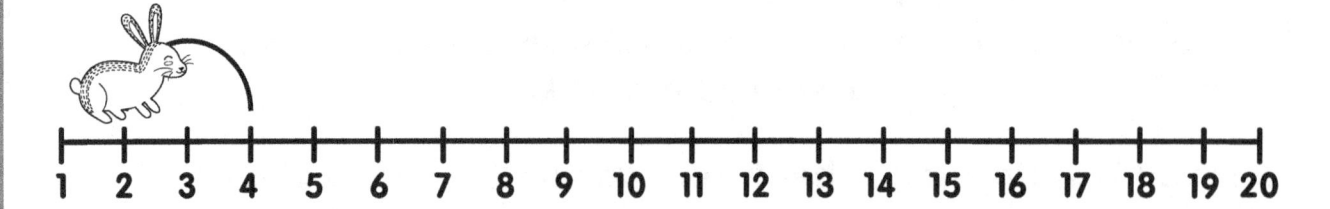

| 1 2 3 4 5 6 7 8 9 10 11 12 13 14 15 16 17 18 19 20

As well as using a number line with hops, we can write the numbers like this:

2,4,6,8,10, ☐

What number should come after 10 in this skip counting pattern?

Skip counting can be a quick way to count up lots of objects.
Each of these art bundles has 5 objects.
Skip count in 5's and write down how many objects there are all together.

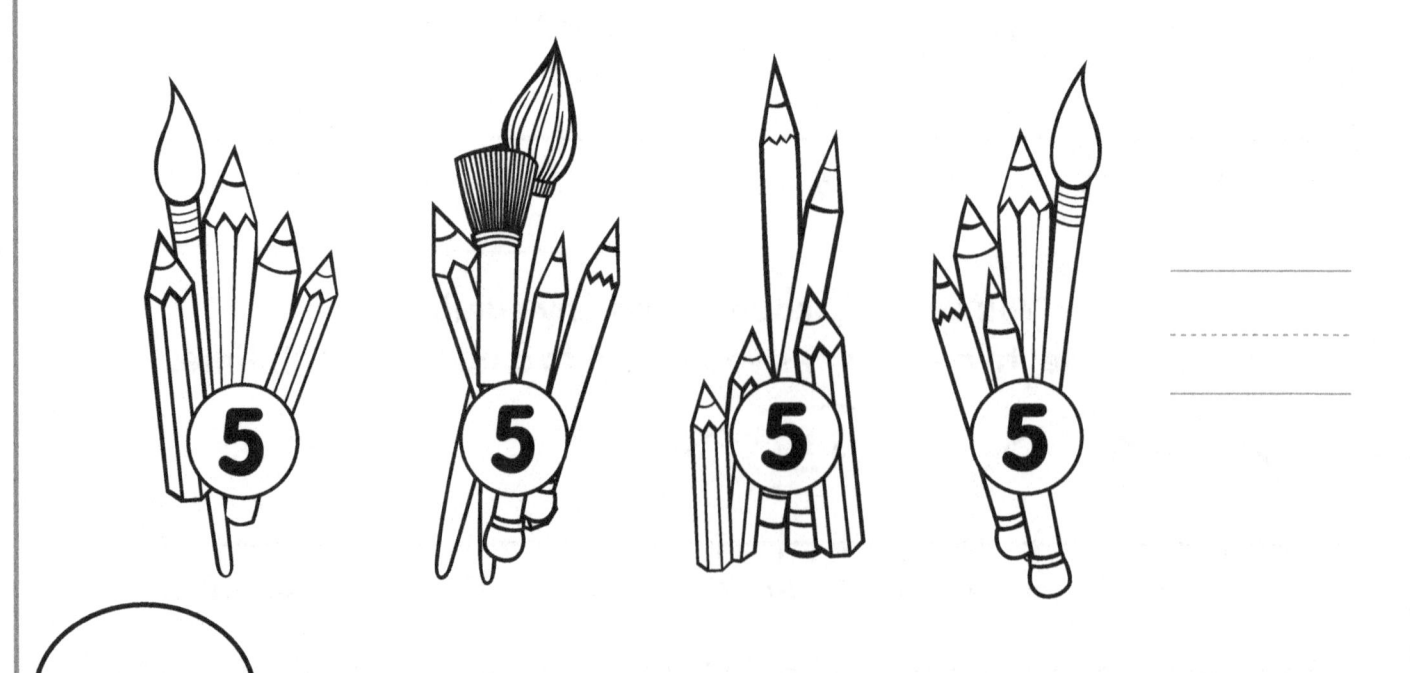

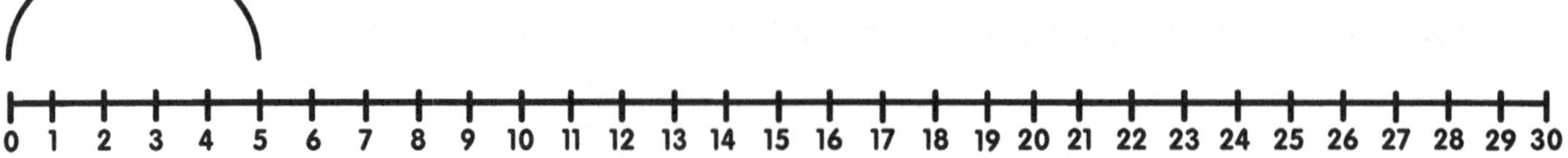

0 1 2 3 4 5 6 7 8 9 10 11 12 13 14 15 16 17 18 19 20 21 22 23 24 25 26 27 28 29 30

Use the number line and draw hops to help you.
The first hop has been done for you.

42

This lighthouse has lots of skip counting numbers missing. Can you fill in the missing numbers?

2 4 _ 8 10 12

25

20

15

_

5

_

3 6 _ 12

There's a number line at the bottom to use if you need it.

0 1 2 3 4 5 6 7 8 9 10 11 12 13 14 15 16 17 18 19 20

43

Fill in the missing hops and numbers.

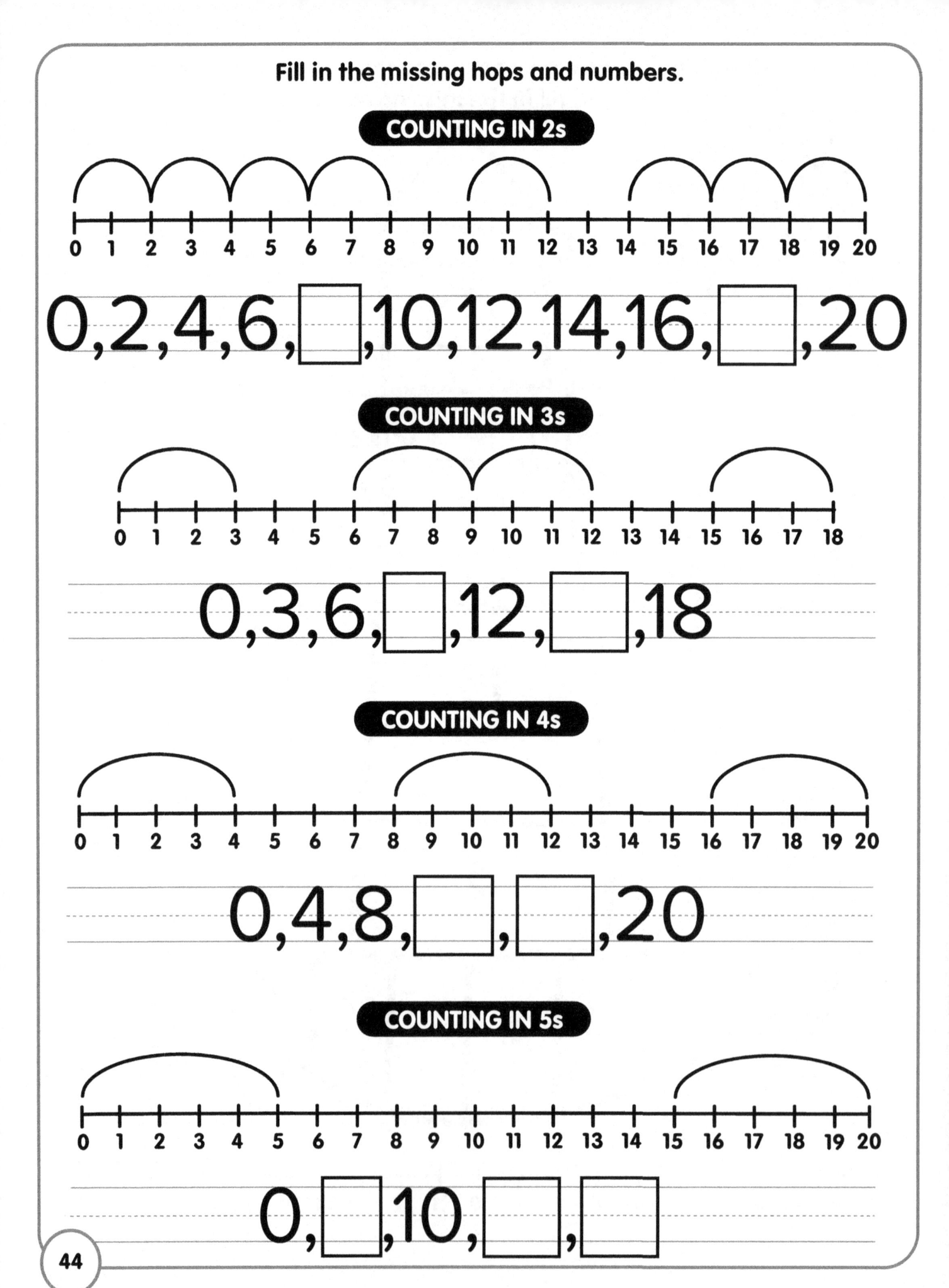

COUNTING IN 2s

0, 2, 4, 6, ☐, 10, 12, 14, 16, ☐, 20

COUNTING IN 3s

0, 3, 6, ☐, 12, ☐, 18

COUNTING IN 4s

0, 4, 8, ☐, ☐, 20

COUNTING IN 5s

0, ☐, 10, ☐, ☐

44

10 Number Bonds
Find the missing number to make the answer 10

Use the dots to help you

7 + 3 = 10

8 + ___ = 10

4 + ___ = 10

___ + 5 = 10

___ + ___ = 10

45

Try without the dots!

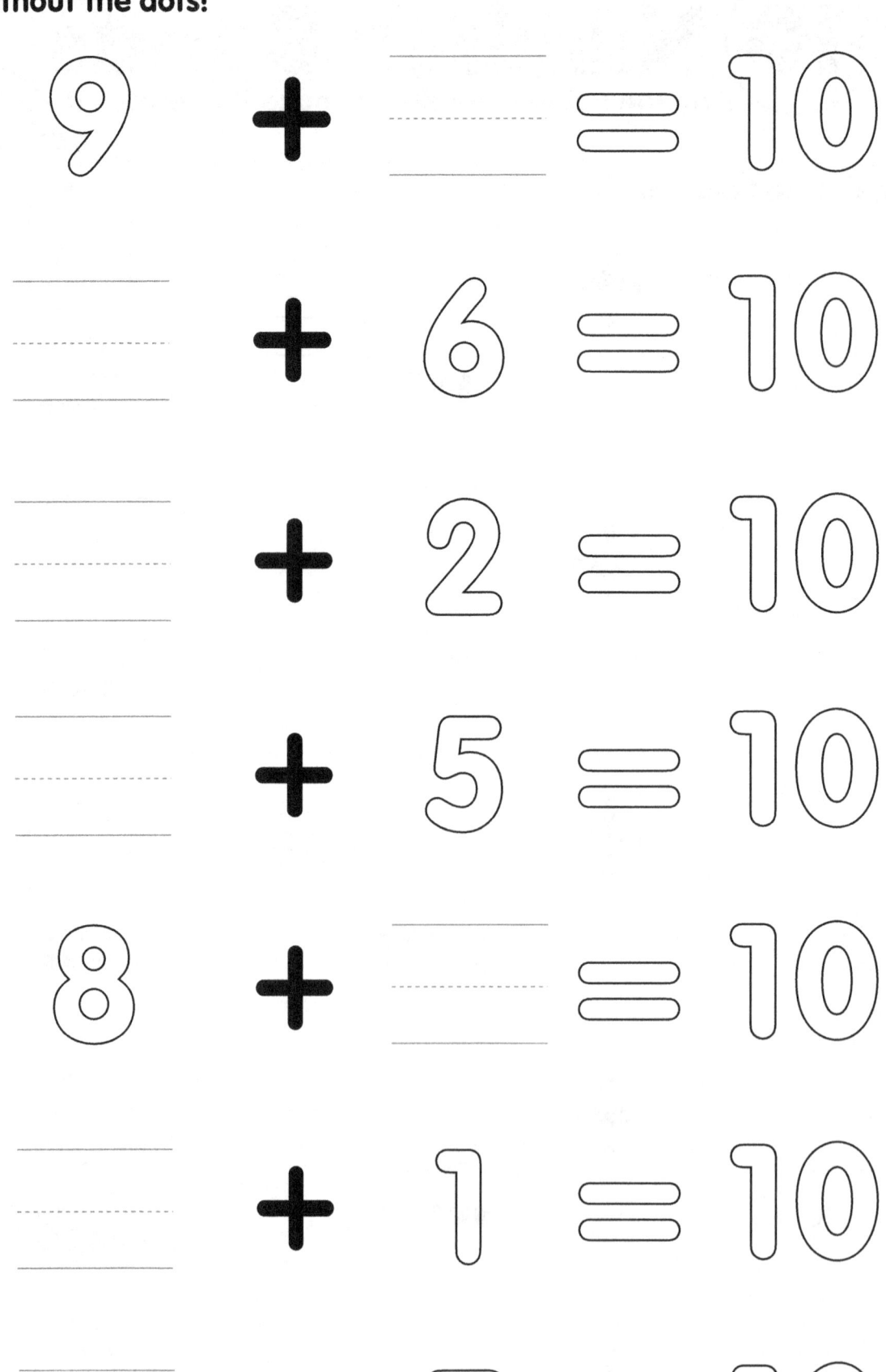

9 + _____ = 10

_____ + 6 = 10

_____ + 2 = 10

_____ + 5 = 10

8 + _____ = 10

_____ + 1 = 10

_____ + 7 = 10

Complete the Number Bond wheel! This number + this number adds up to 10.

Choose any 2 numbers that add up to 10!

SUPER STAR CHALLENGE!

47

Can you find the missing numbers to add up to 10?

DRAW YOUR ANSWER
ANY OBJECTS YOU LIKE!

48

20 Number Bonds
Find the missing number to make the answer 20

Use the dots to help you.

12 + ___ = 20

7 + ___ = 20

15 + ___ = 20

___ + 4 = 20

___ + ___ = 20

49

Try without the dots!

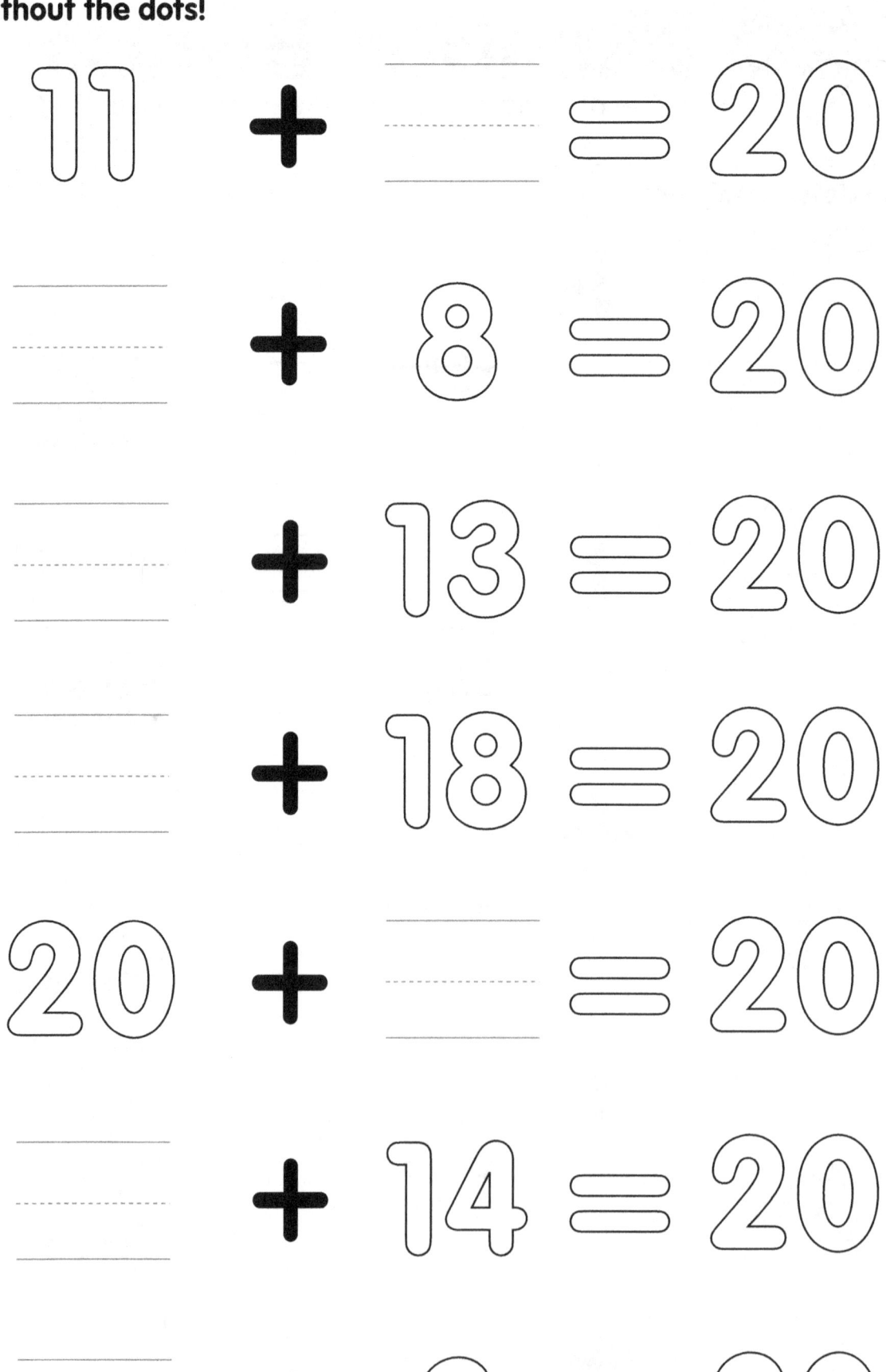

11 + ___ = 20

___ + 8 = 20

___ + 13 = 20

___ + 18 = 20

20 + ___ = 20

___ + 14 = 20

___ + 3 = 20

Complete the Number Bond wheel! This number + this number adds up to 20.

- 11
- 13
- 9
- 7
- 8
- 12
- 20
- 5
- 10
- 1
- 6
- 14
- 15

Choose any 2 numbers that add up to 20!

SUPER STAR CHALLENGE!

51

Can you find the missing numbers to add up to 10?

DRAW YOUR ANSWER

ANY SHAPES YOU LIKE!

Color and Count!

How many of each ice cream can you find?
Write your answers in the circles at the bottom of the page.

ICE CREAM

WRITE THE TOTALS OF EACH ICE CREAM IN THE CIRCLES HERE!

Color and Count!

How many of each item can you find?
Write your answers in the circles at the bottom of the page.

WRITE THE TOTALS OF EACH ITEM IN THE CIRCLES HERE!

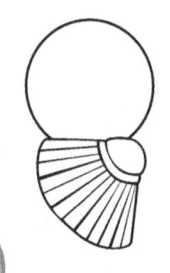

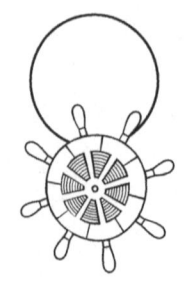

Color and Count!

How many of each object can you find?
Write your answers in the circles at the bottom of the page.

BACK TO SCHOOL

WRITE THE TOTALS OF EACH ITEM IN THE CIRCLES HERE!

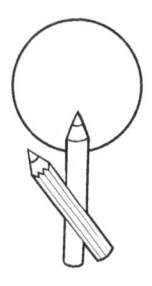

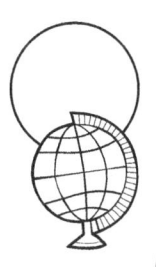

55

Color and Count!

How many of each object can you find?
Write your answers in the circles at the bottom of the page.

TRAVEL TIME

WRITE THE TOTALS OF EACH ITEM IN THE CIRCLES HERE!

56

Color and Count!

How many of each object can you find?
Write your answers in the circles at the bottom of the page.

WRITE THE TOTALS OF EACH ITEM IN THE CIRCLES HERE!

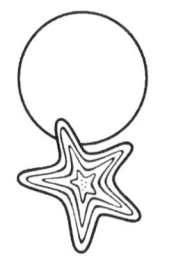

57

Number Patterns

What numbers are missing? Write them in the boxes.

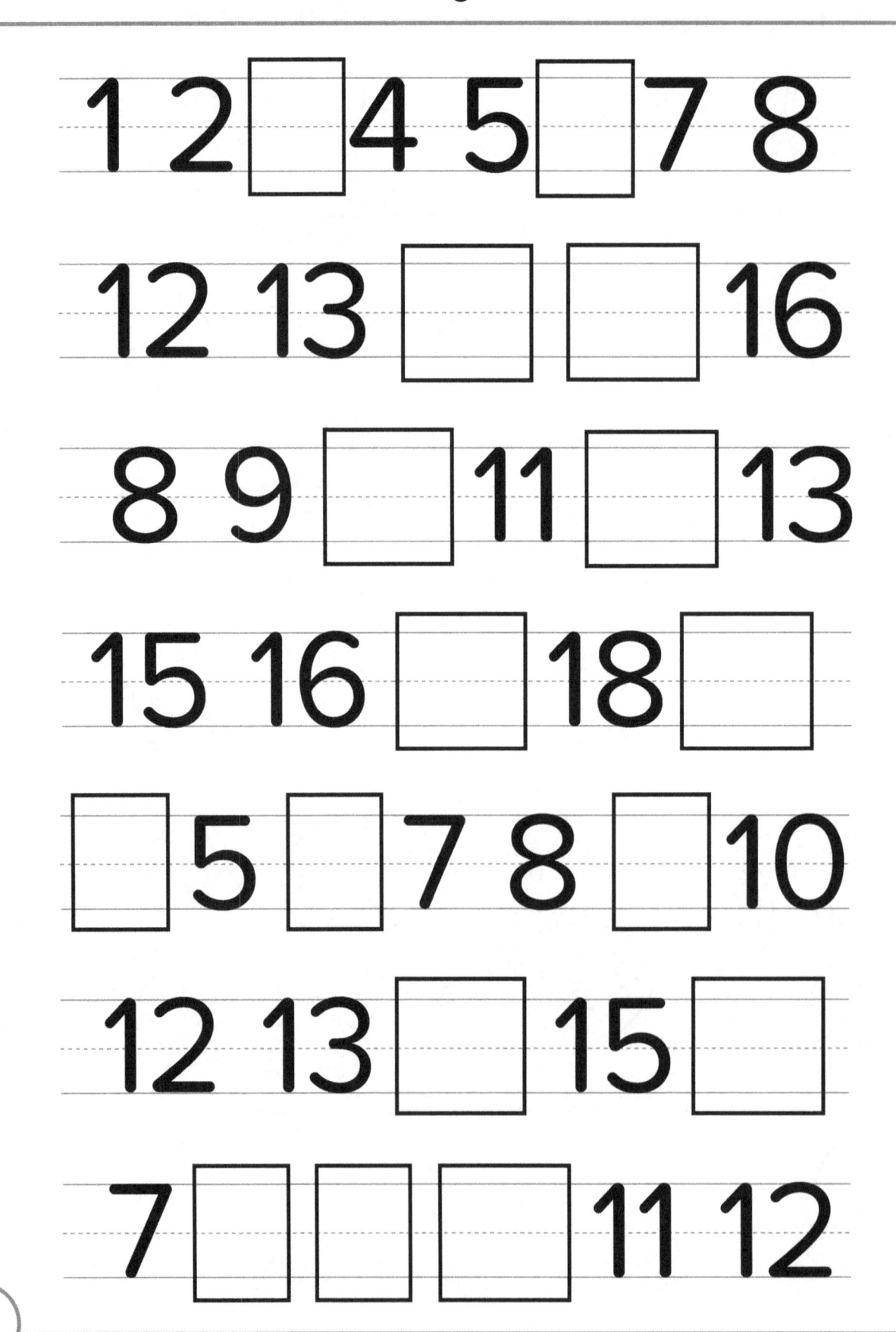

1 2 [3] 4 5 [6] 7 8

12 13 [14] [15] 16

8 9 [10] 11 [12] 13

15 16 [17] 18 [19]

[4] 5 [6] 7 8 [9] 10

12 13 [14] 15 [16]

7 [8] [9] [10] 11 12

Follow the pattern, what numbers are missing? Write them in the boxes.

2　4　[ ]　8　10　[ ]　14

10　12　[ ]　16　[ ]　20

8　[ ]　[ ]　14　[ ]　18　20

4　6　8　[ ]　[ ]　[ ]

Start at 0, follow the number pattern and paths to get to the fish. What numbers are missing? Write them in the boxes.

0　[ ]　4　[ ]　[ ]　10

8

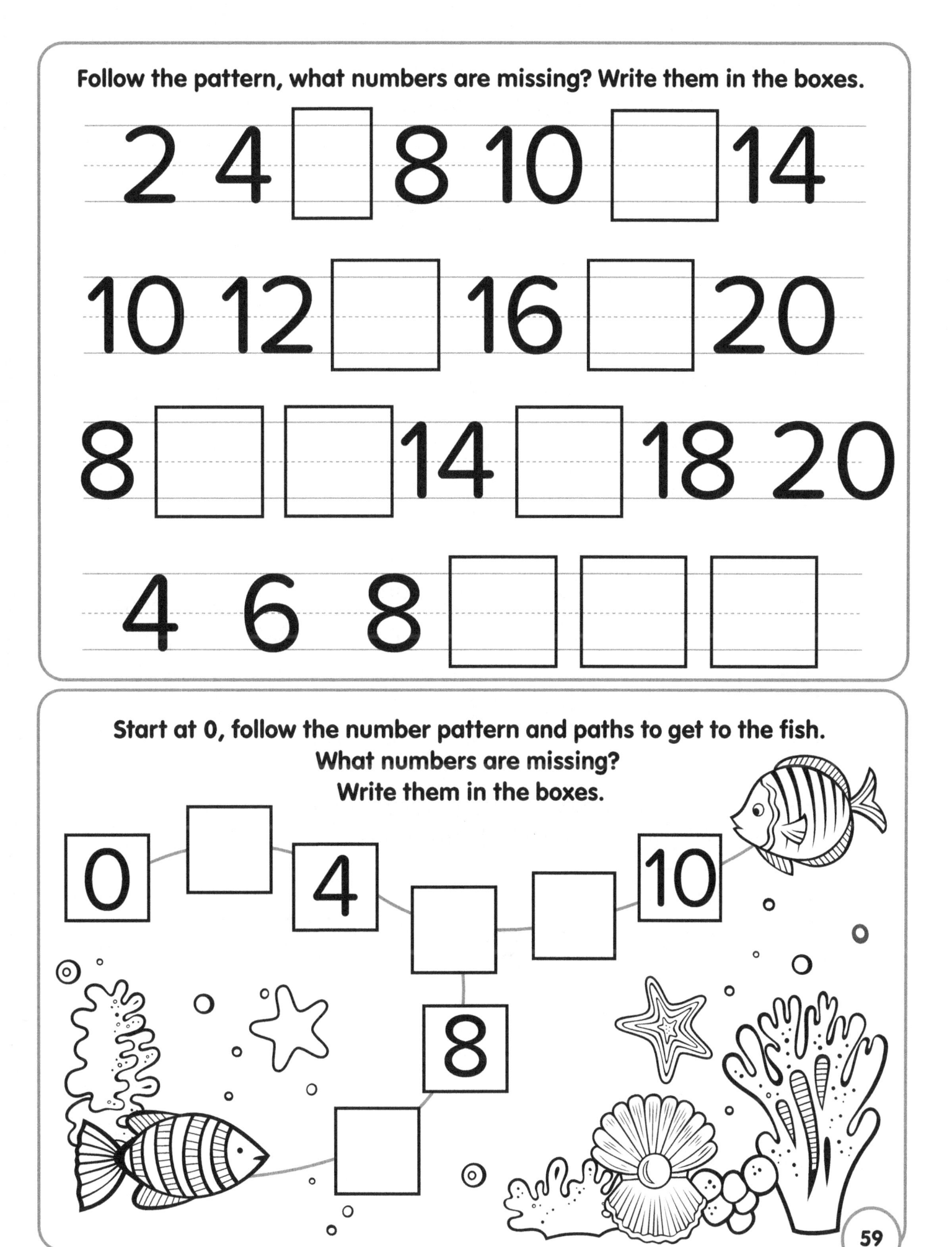

Count the objects and write the numbers of each in the boxes. There's a number pattern, what number comes next?

WHAT NUMBER COMES NEXT?

WHAT NUMBER COMES NEXT?

Follow the line and number pattern. What numbers are missing? Write them in the boxes.

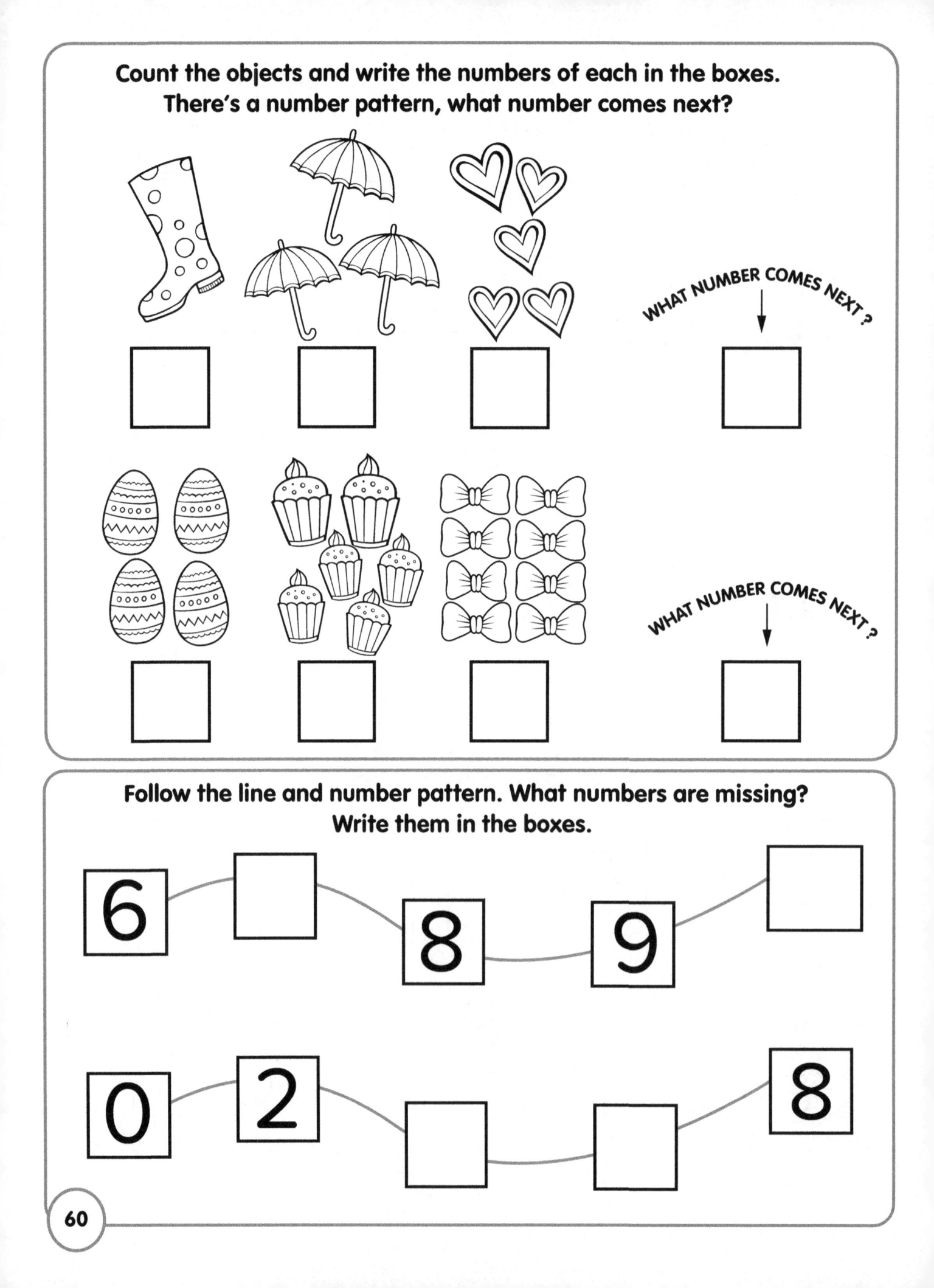

6 ☐ 8 9 ☐

0 2 ☐ ☐ 8

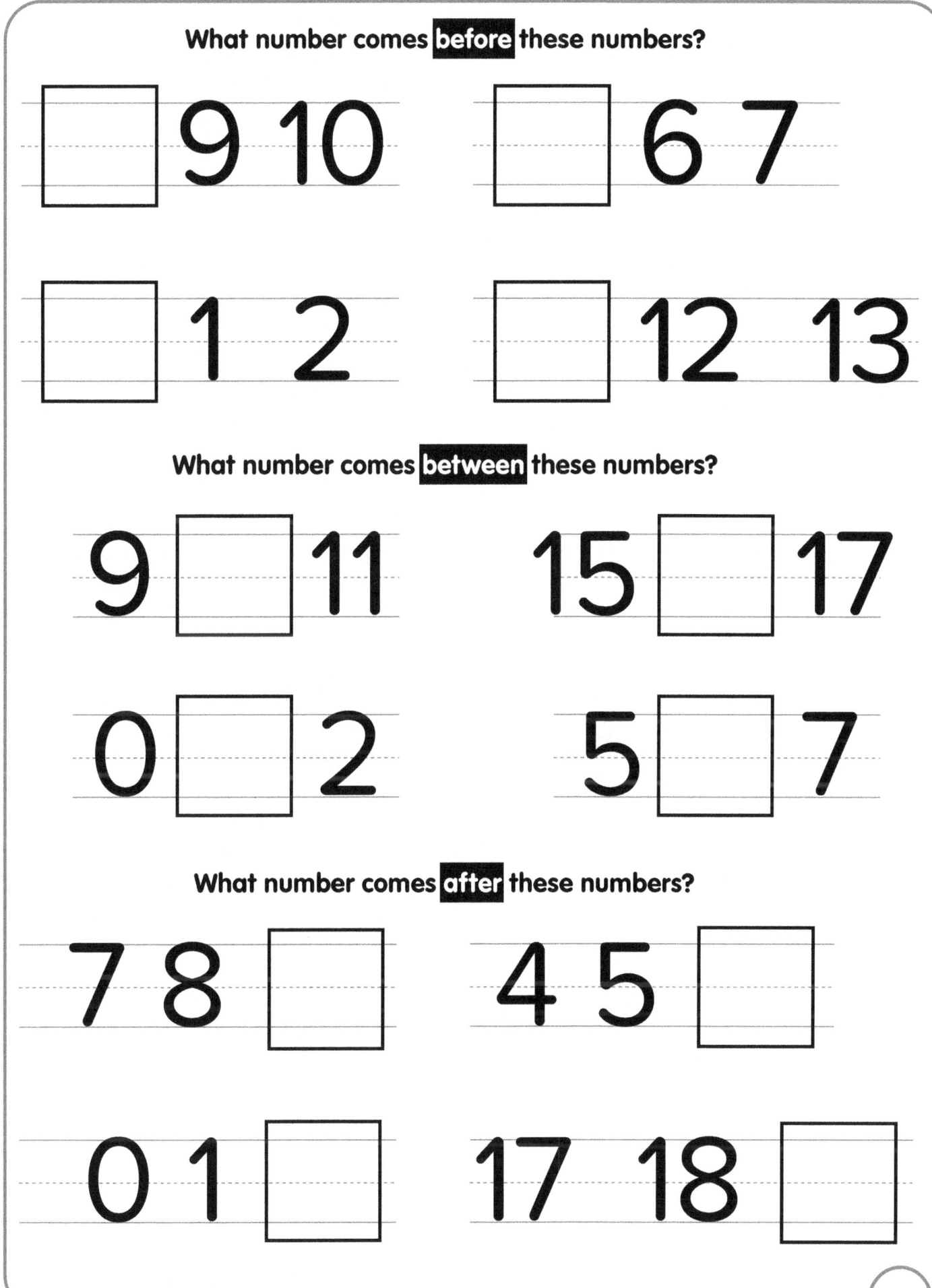

What number comes before these numbers?

☐ 9 10   ☐ 6 7

☐ 1 2   ☐ 12 13

What number comes between these numbers?

9 ☐ 11   15 ☐ 17

0 ☐ 2   5 ☐ 7

What number comes after these numbers?

7 8 ☐   4 5 ☐

0 1 ☐   17 18 ☐

Ordinal Numbers

Ordinal numbers tell us the position of an object in a list

Here are 4 birds. They are lined up waiting for their lunch!

1st 2nd 3rd 4th

This bird is at the front, she is 1st and will get her lunch before all the others.

This bird is next, she is 2nd.

This bird is next, she is 3rd.

This bird is at the back, she is 4th and will get her lunch after all the others.

Here are 6 cats waiting for dinner, circle the one that is 3rd.
Color the 5th cat red.

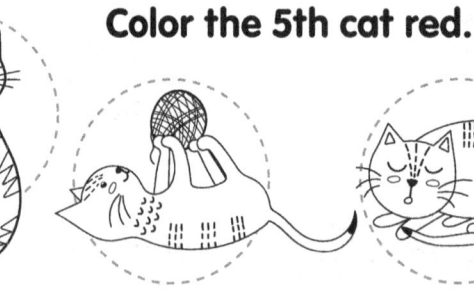

Circle the animal in the 2nd truck.

62

Every number position can have an ordinal number.

If you are in position **1** then you are **1st**	If you are in position **2** then you are **2nd**	If you are in position **3** then you are **3rd**	If you are in position **4** then you are **4th**	If you are in position **5** then you are **5th**

If you are in position _____

then you are _____

What would be your next position and number?

1st

What shape is on the 7th fish?   ☆   or   ◯

Which position fish has the ☐ shape? _____

Which position fish is missing a shape? _____

What shape is on the 8th fish?   ☆   or   ◯

A group of owls are waiting for a taxi.
Add the missing position numbers under each one.

2nd   **4th**

Circle the owl that gets in the taxi last.

This monster finished 3rd in a pizza eating competition.

How many monsters finished in front of him? ____

Circle the dino egg that has hatched 1st.

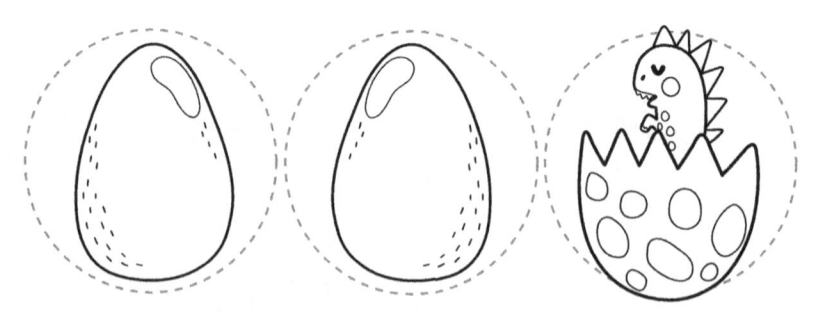

Color the 5th circle blue.
Color the 8th circle green.
Color the 3rd circle red.

What position would the next monster be? ____

Each of these stars have dots inside.
Add the dots together from the 5th and 8th star.

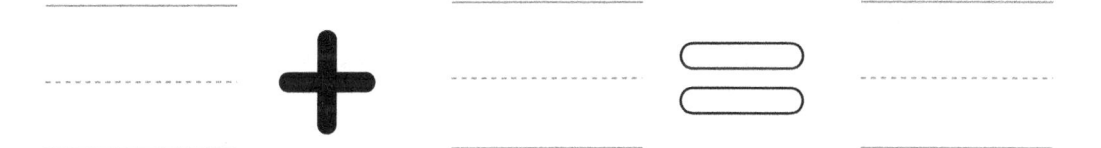

____ + ____ = ____

Use this chart whenever you need it.
It shows all the ordinal numbers from 1-20.

1	2	3	4	5	6	7	8	9	10
1st	2nd	3rd	4th	5th	6th	7th	8th	9th	10th
11	12	13	14	15	16	17	18	19	20
11th	12th	13th	14th	15th	16th	17th	18th	19th	20th

Shapes

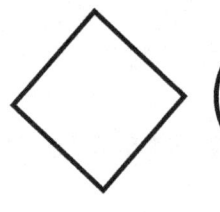

Trace and draw the shapes, start at the star!
How many sides does each shape have?

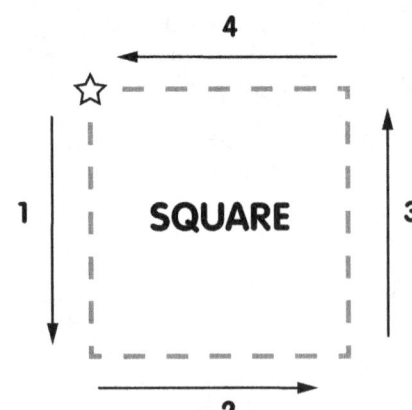

A square has _____ sides.

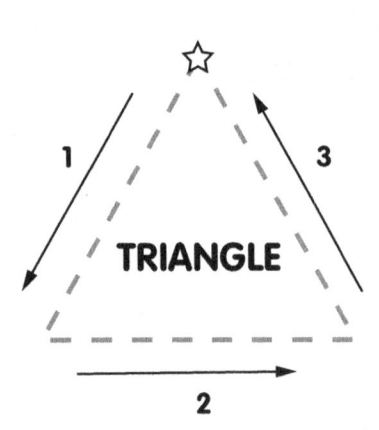

A triangle has _____ sides.

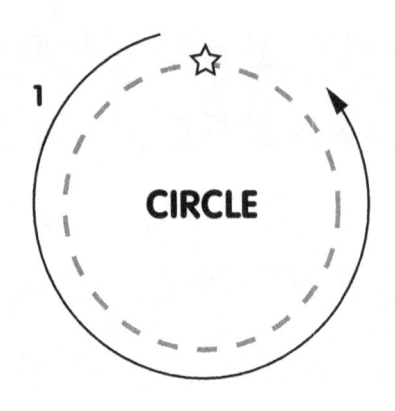

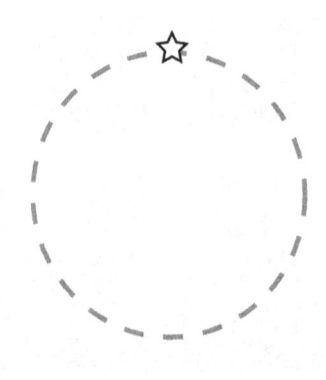

A circle has _____ side.

RECTANGLE

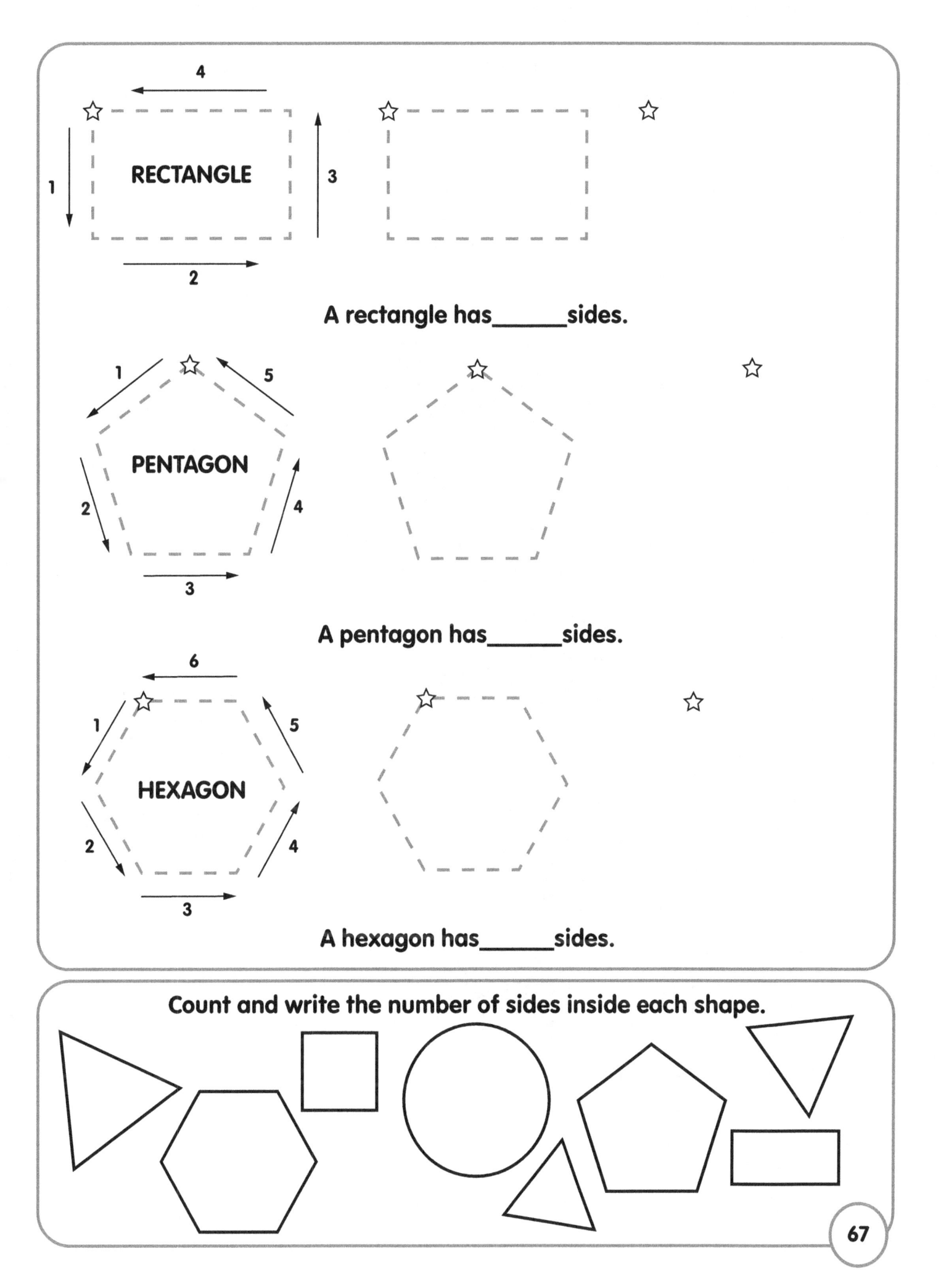

A rectangle has _____ sides.

PENTAGON

A pentagon has _____ sides.

HEXAGON

A hexagon has _____ sides.

Count and write the number of sides inside each shape.

**Color in each type of shape in a different color.
You might choose to color all the circles in red and all the triangles in green.
It's up to you!**

How many of each shape did you find hiding between the leaves?
Write your answer inside the shapes below.

68

Color in each type of shape in a different color.
You might choose to color all the circles in blue and all the triangles in yellow.

Which shape comes next in the pattern. Color the correct answer.

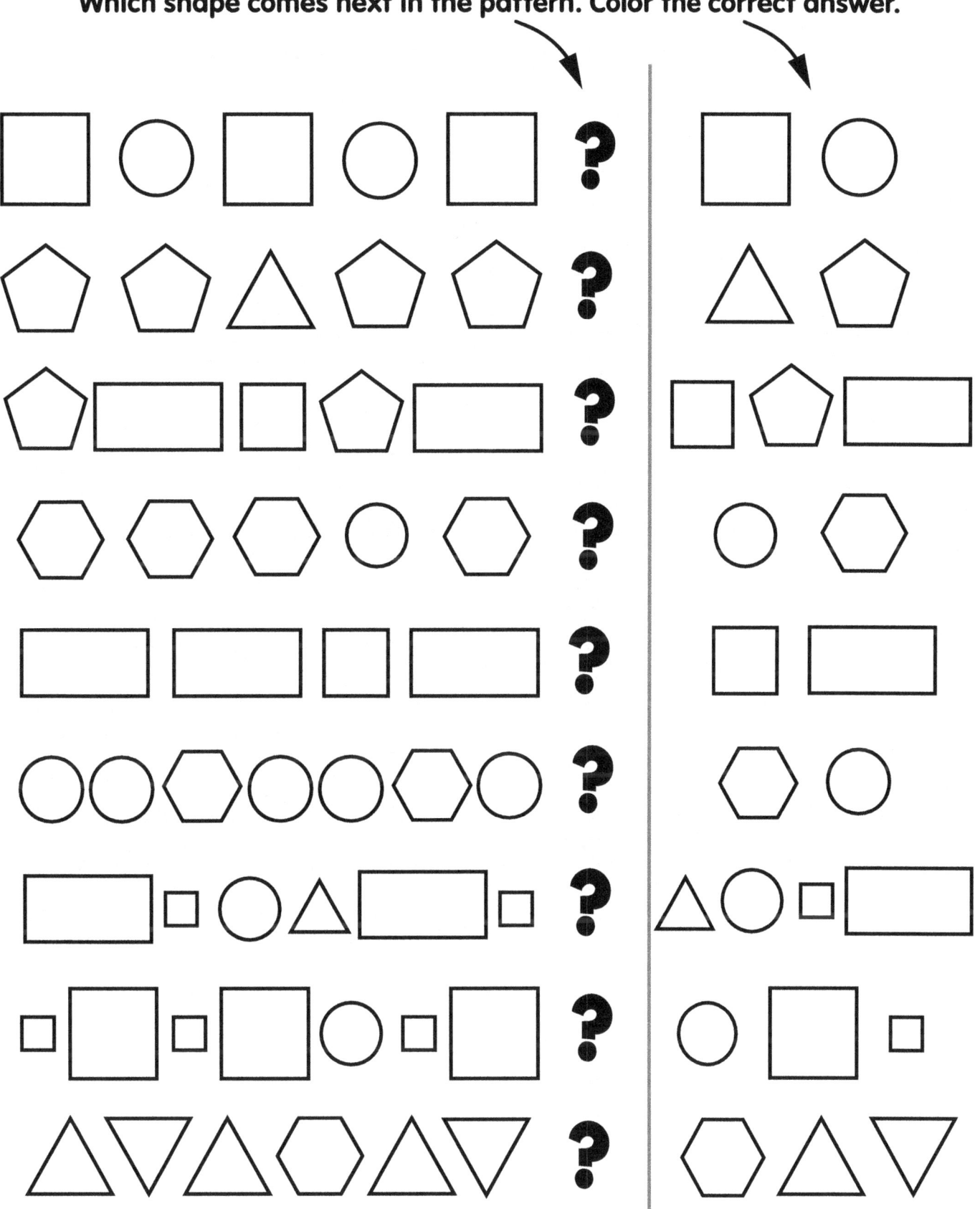

More and Less

Count each type of animal and write the number underneath.
Which animal is there **more** of?

_____   _____

There are more: Circle the correct answer.

_____   _____

There are more: Circle the correct answer.

70

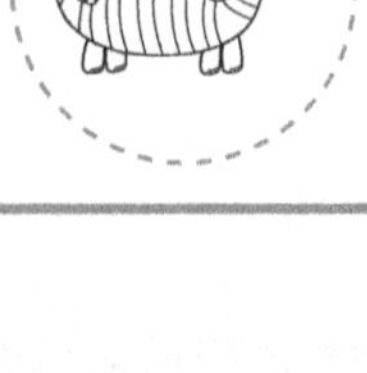

**Count each type of animal and write the number underneath.
Which animal is there more of?**

There are more: 　　　　　Circle the correct answer.

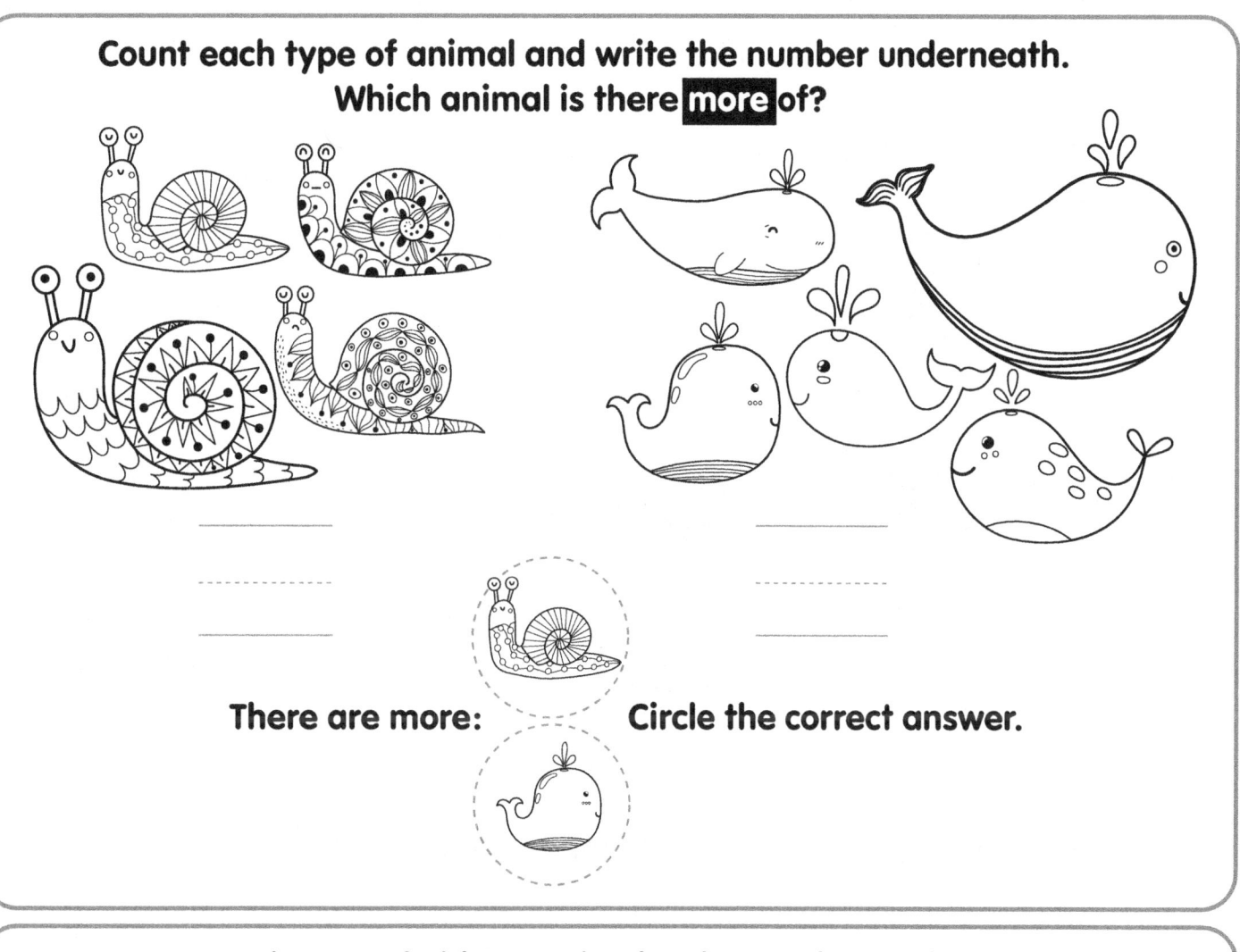

Count each type of object and write the number underneath.

is 　**MORE** / **LESS** 　than

Circle whether the first number is MORE or LESS than the second number.

Count each type of object and write the number underneath.

_____ is **MORE** / **LESS** than _____

Circle whether the first number is MORE or LESS than the second number.

11 is **MORE** / **LESS** than 9

17 is **MORE** / **LESS** than 18

9 is **MORE** / **LESS** than 8

19 is **MORE** / **LESS** than 9

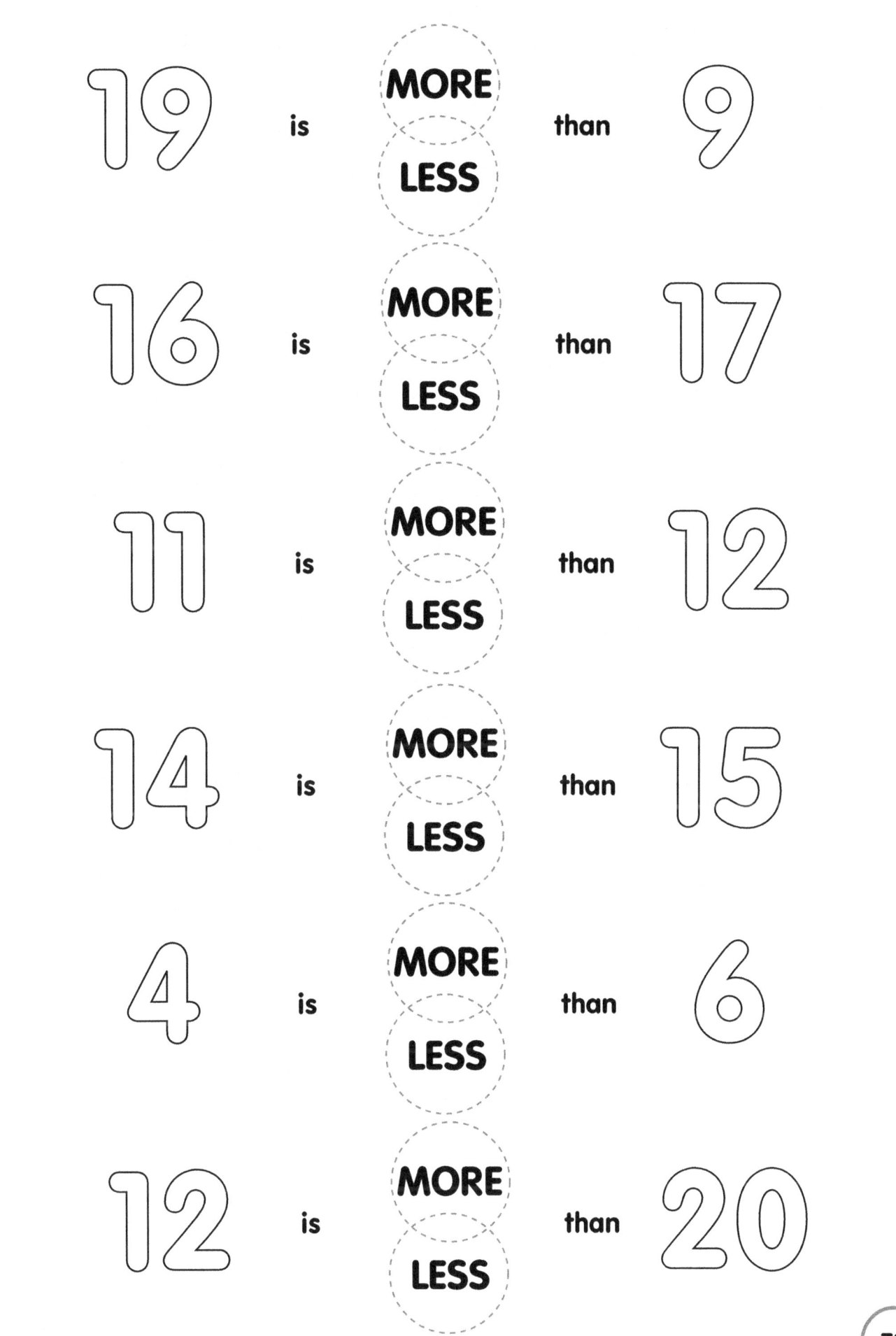

16 is **MORE** / **LESS** than 17

11 is **MORE** / **LESS** than 12

14 is **MORE** / **LESS** than 15

4 is **MORE** / **LESS** than 6

12 is **MORE** / **LESS** than 20

Odd and Even

ODD numbers end with a 1,3,5,7 or 9
EVEN numbers end with a 2,4,6,8 or 0

What a mess of numbers! Can you color in just the EVEN numbers?

2 1 6 9 1 4
9 7 4 8 3 9 7
4 5 10 6 5

Another mess of numbers! Can you color in just the ODD numbers?

9 5 8 1 4 5
2 1 9 7 10 9
6 7 4 3 6 4

74

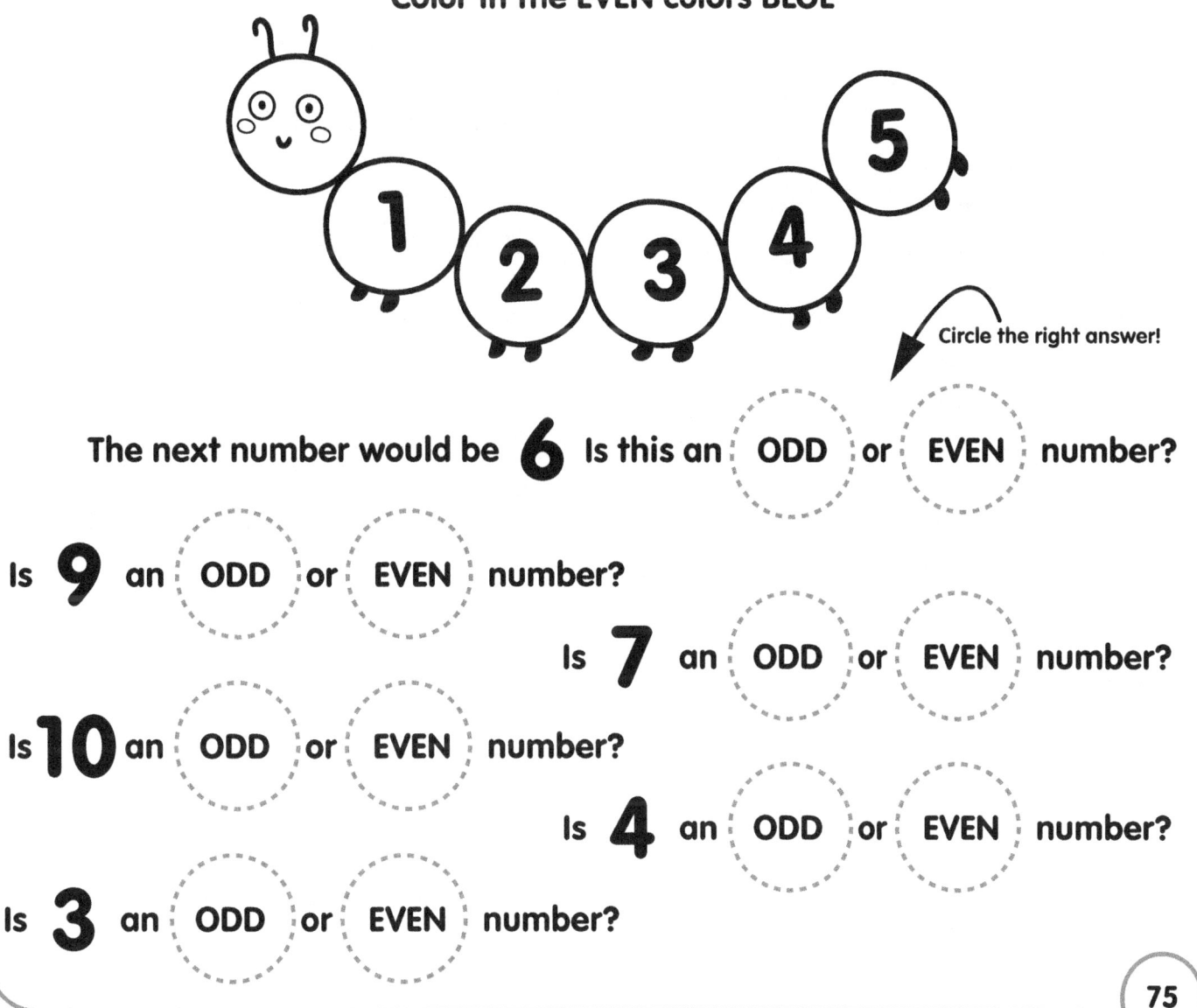

**Color in the ODD numbers on the caterpillar RED.
Color in the EVEN colors BLUE**

Write in the missing number and color it in the right color.

**Color in the ODD numbers on the caterpillar RED.
Color in the EVEN colors BLUE**

Circle the right answer!

The next number would be **6** Is this an ODD or EVEN number?

Is **9** an ODD or EVEN number?

Is **7** an ODD or EVEN number?

Is **10** an ODD or EVEN number?

Is **4** an ODD or EVEN number?

Is **3** an ODD or EVEN number?

Every number is either ODD or EVEN, really big numbers too!
Color in the EVEN numbers in green.
Color in the ODD numbers in yellow.

REMEMBER ODD numbers end with a 1,3,5,7 or 9.
EVEN numbers end with a 2,4,6,8 or 0.

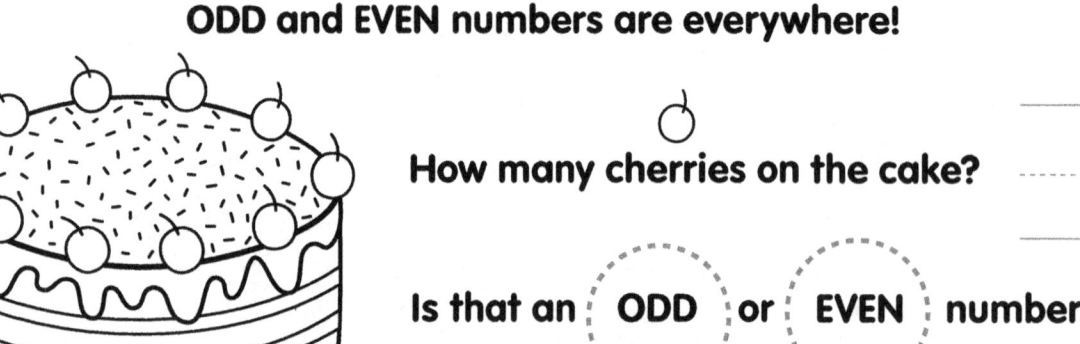

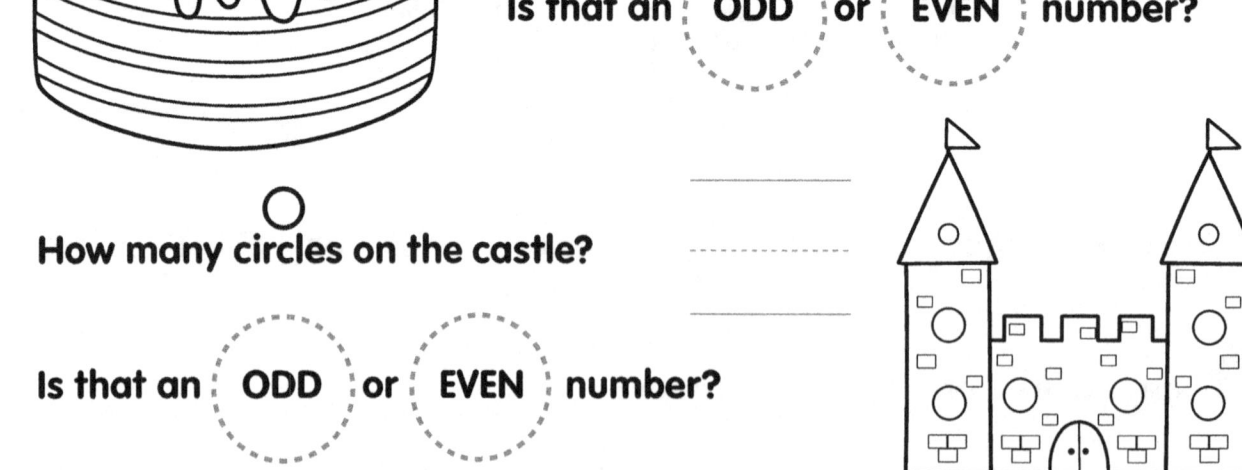

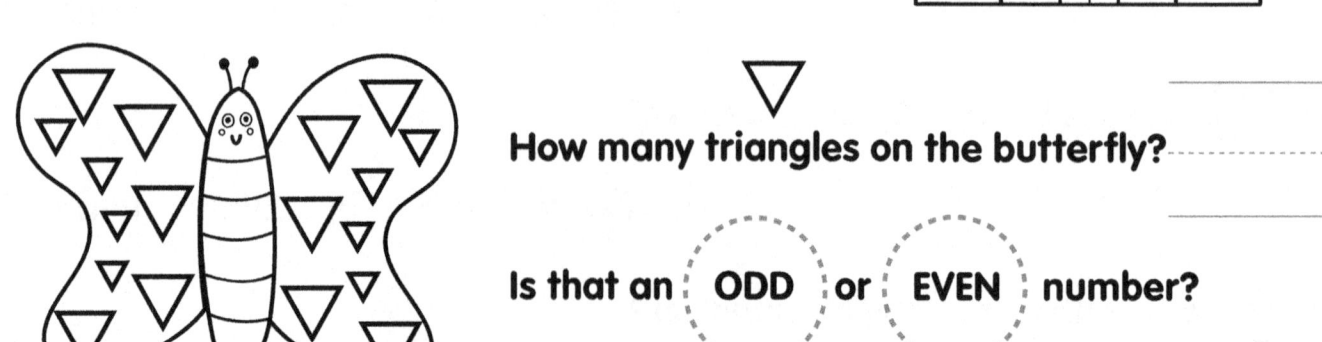

19   28   46   100
21   33   67

ODD and EVEN numbers are everywhere!

How many cherries on the cake? _____

Is that an (ODD) or (EVEN) number?

How many circles on the castle? _____

Is that an (ODD) or (EVEN) number?

How many triangles on the butterfly? _____

Is that an (ODD) or (EVEN) number?

76

Left and Right

Color in the pumpkin on the RIGHT.

Circle the pizza on the LEFT.

Circle the bird on the LEFT.

Color in the cake on the RIGHT.

Count the pasta shapes and write the number on each side below.

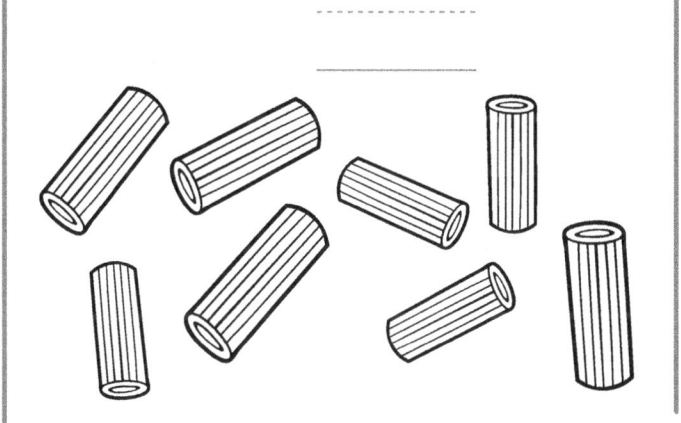

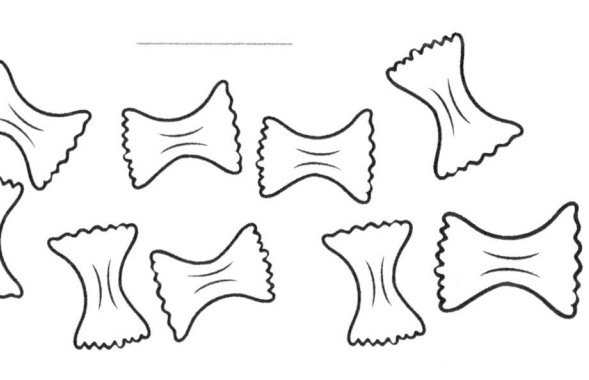

Is there more pasta on the LEFT or RIGHT ?

77

Which side equals more?

3 + 4 | 8 − 2

LEFT   or   RIGHT

1 + 5 | 9 − 4

LEFT   or   RIGHT

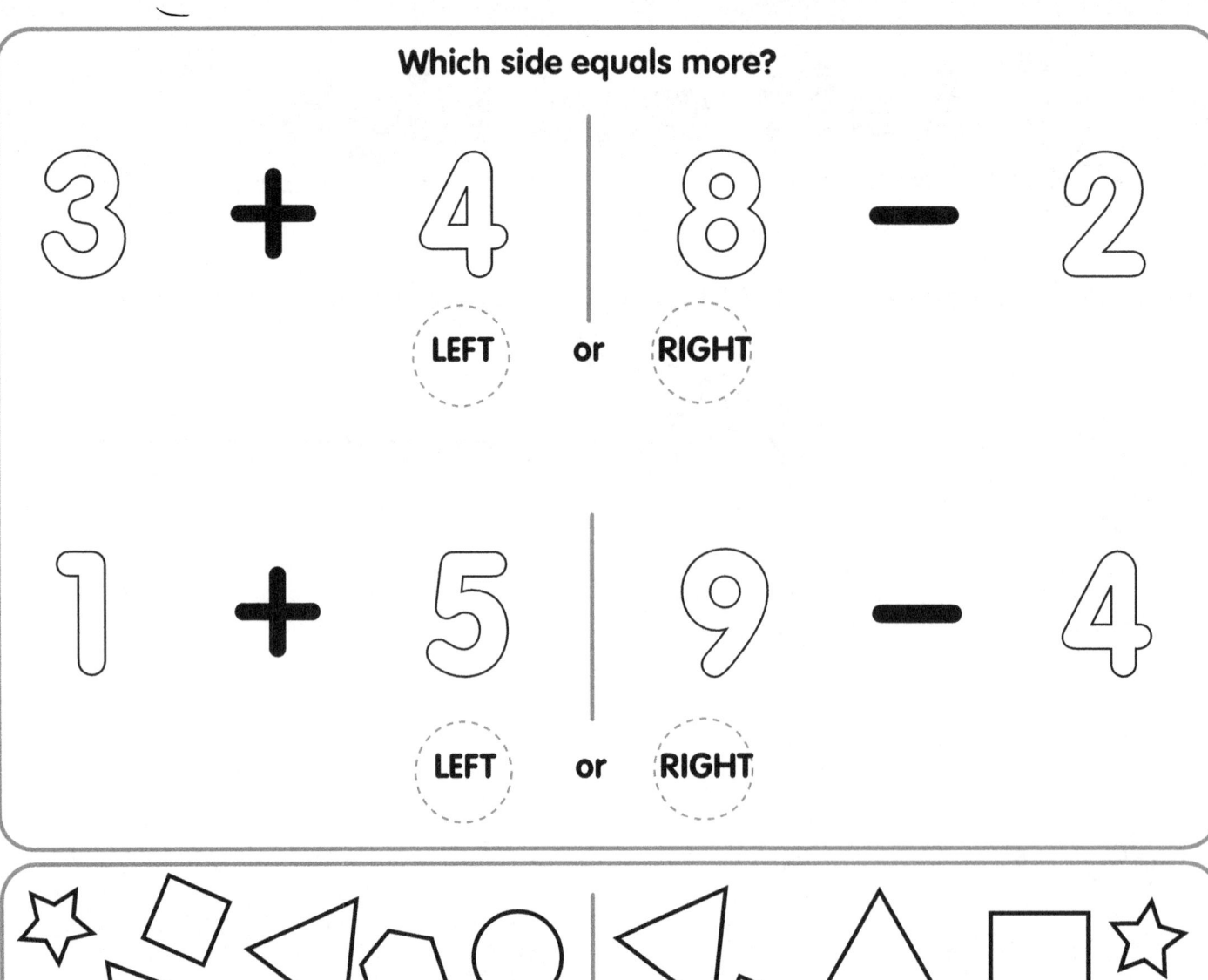

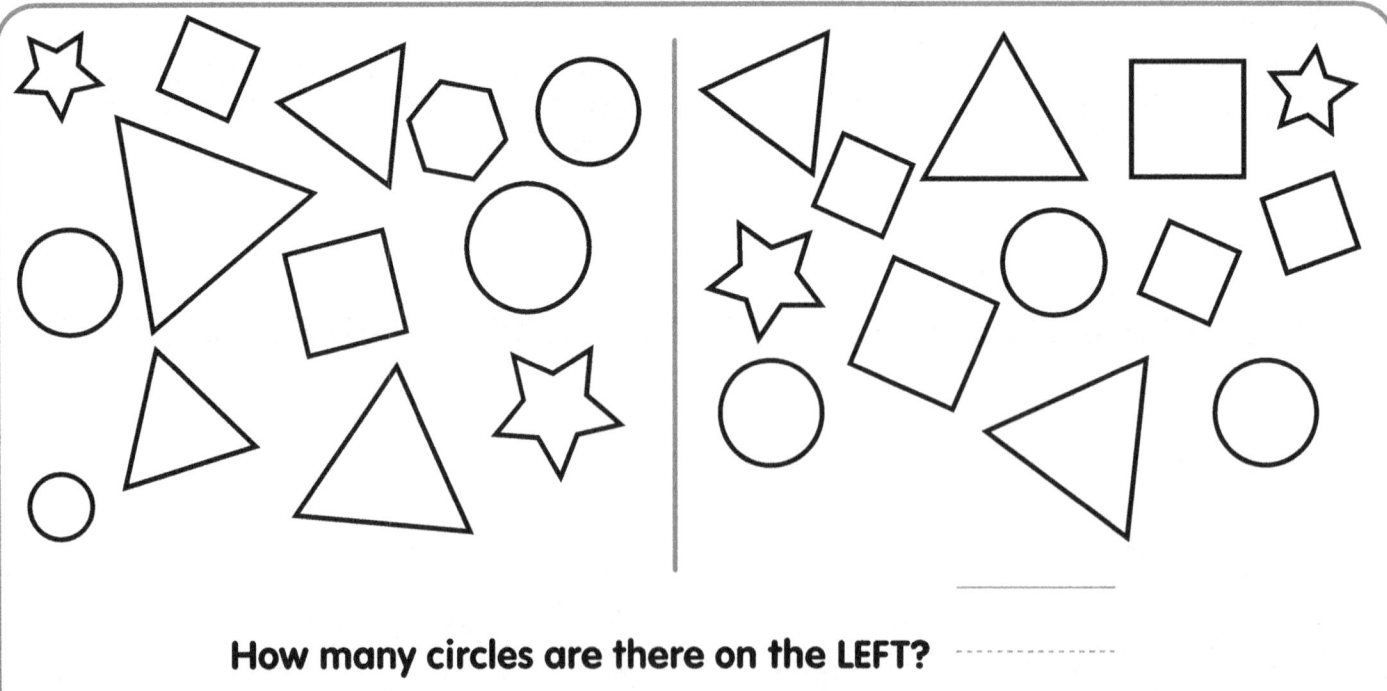

How many circles are there on the LEFT? _____

Are there more squares on the LEFT or RIGHT ?

Are there more triangles on the LEFT or RIGHT ?

78

Bigger and Smaller

Which is bigger? Circle the BIGGER animal.

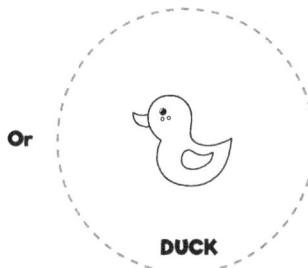

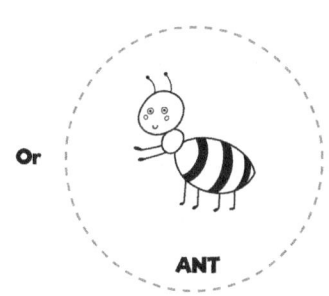

DINOSAUR Or DUCK

BUTTERFLY Or ELEPHANT

CAT Or ANT

COW Or BIRD

Elephant and Bird are best friends. Which one is BIGGER?

Which planet is BIGGER?

Which cake is BIGGER?

79

Which is smaller? Circle the SMALLER object.

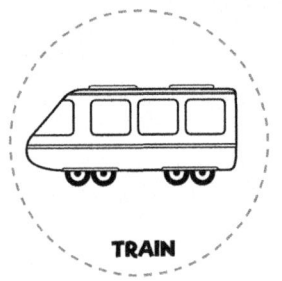

TRAIN Or MOTORBIKE

BIKE Or TRACTOR

These 2 wolves are sisters.
Which one is SMALLER?

Which whale is SMALLER?

Which flower is SMALLER?

Which ice cream is SMALLER?

Sometimes we have more than 2 objects and we need to say which is the BIGGEST or SMALLEST.
The BIGGEST is the object that is BIGGER than all the others.
The SMALLEST is the object that is SMALLER than all the others.

Which fish is the BIGGEST?

Which star is the BIGGEST?

Which fish is the SMALLEST?

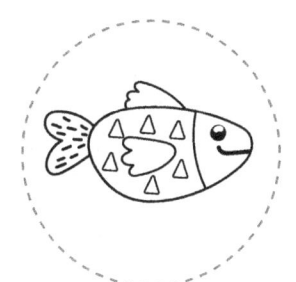

Which star is the SMALLEST?

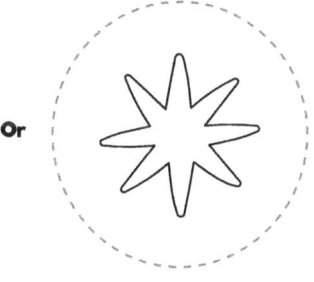

81

Here is a picture of an apple. Draw and color a BIGGER apple here.

Here is a picture of a flower. Draw and color a SMALLER flower here.

Draw a square here that would be the BIGGEST square.

Draw a triangle here that would be the SMALLEST triangle.

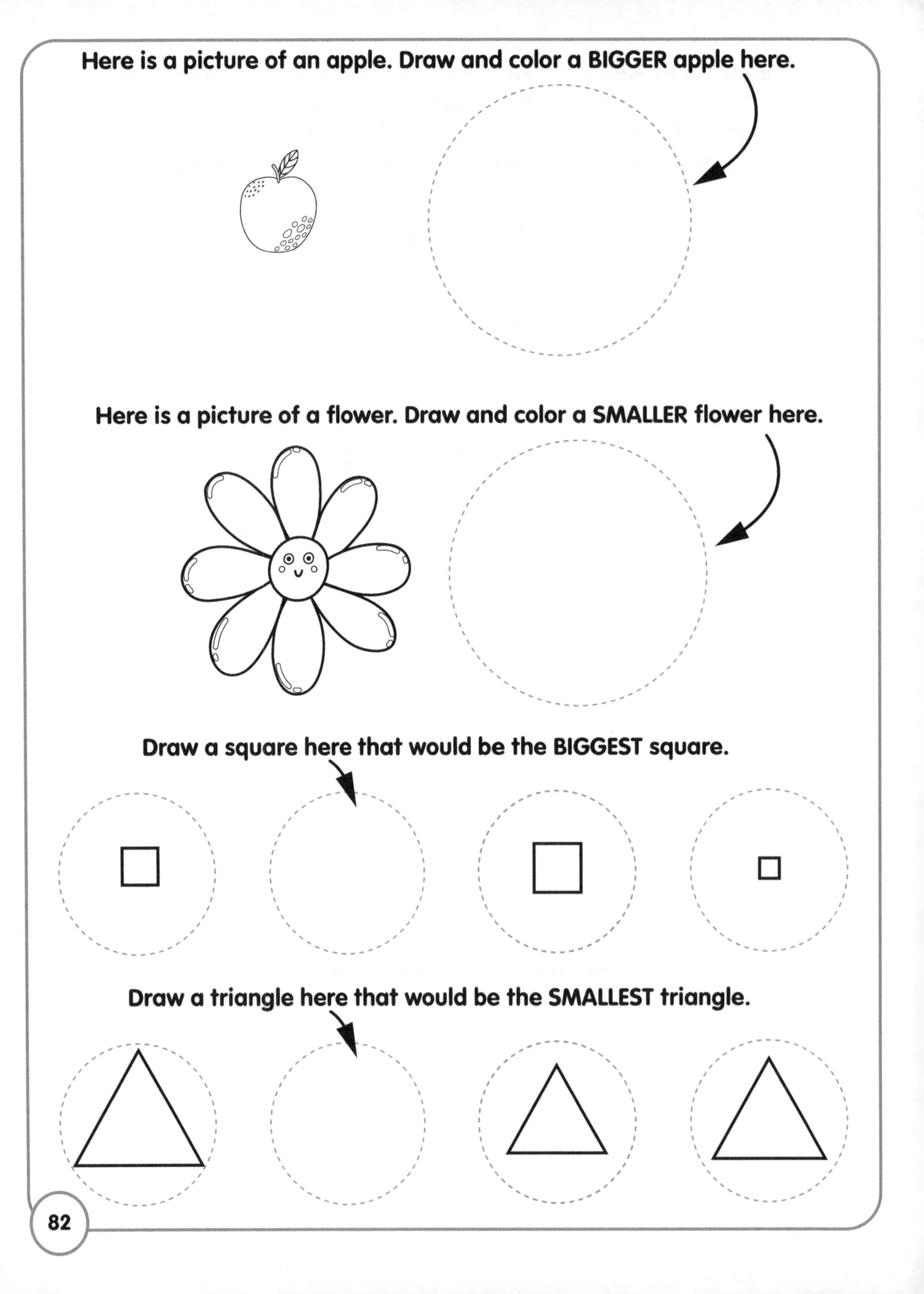

82

Longer and Shorter

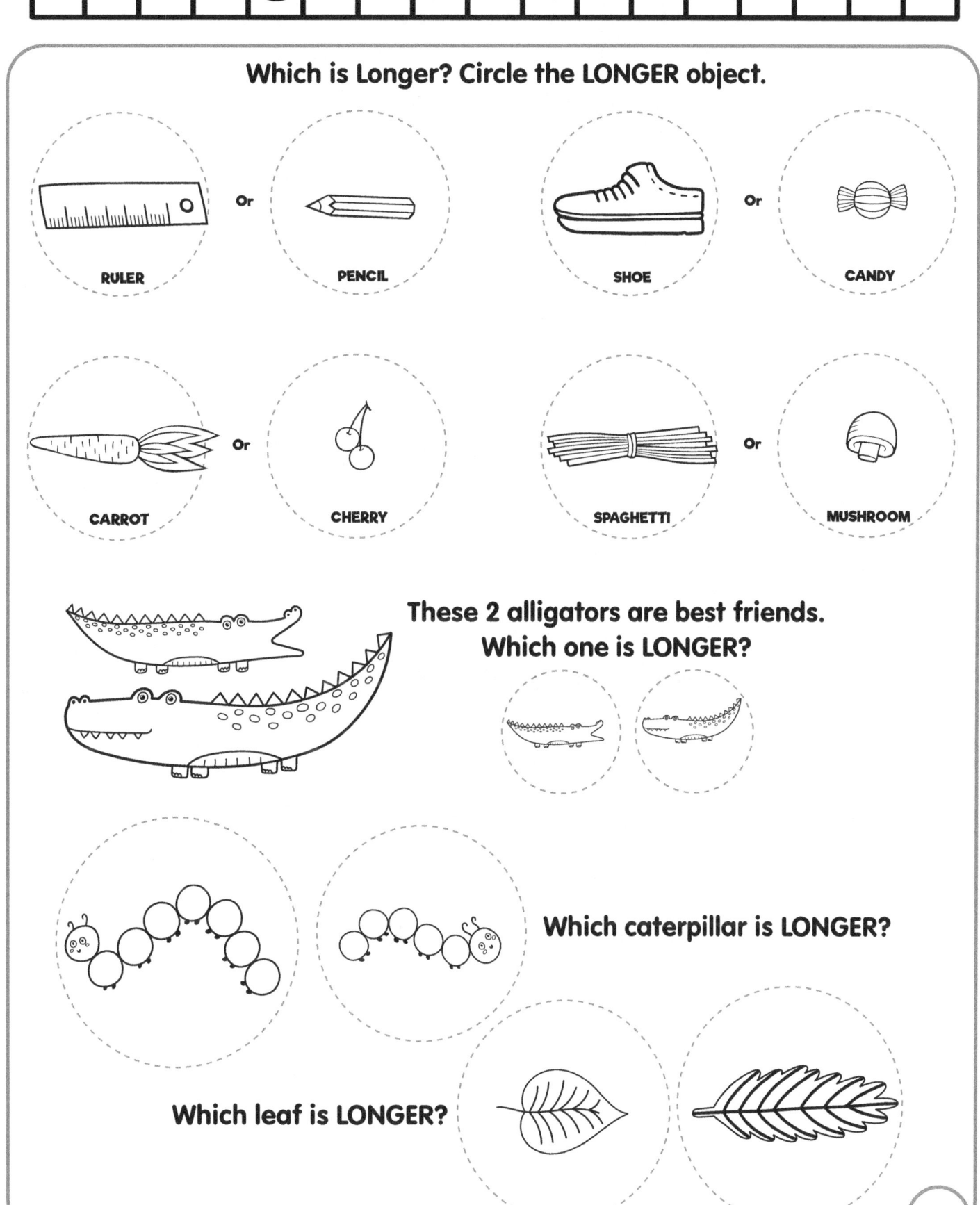

Which is Longer? Circle the LONGER object.

| RULER | Or | PENCIL | | SHOE | Or | CANDY |

| CARROT | Or | CHERRY | | SPAGHETTI | Or | MUSHROOM |

These 2 alligators are best friends.
Which one is LONGER?

Which caterpillar is LONGER?

Which leaf is LONGER?

Sometimes we have more than 2 objects and we need to say which is the LONGEST or SHORTEST.
The LONGEST is the object that is LONGER than all the others.
The SHORTEST is the object that is SHORTER than all the others.

Which pencil is the LONGEST?

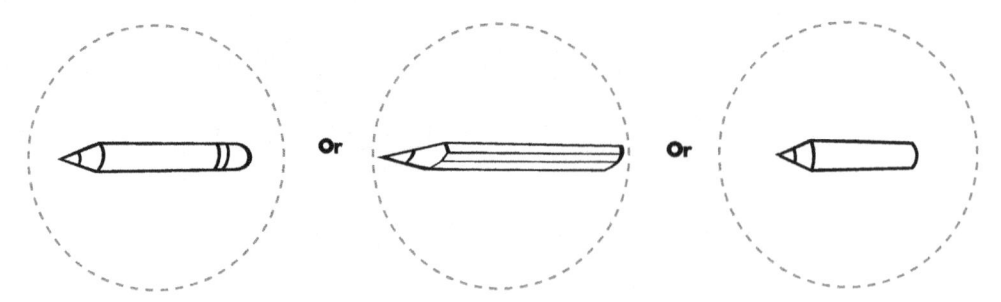

Or   Or

Which arrow is the LONGEST?

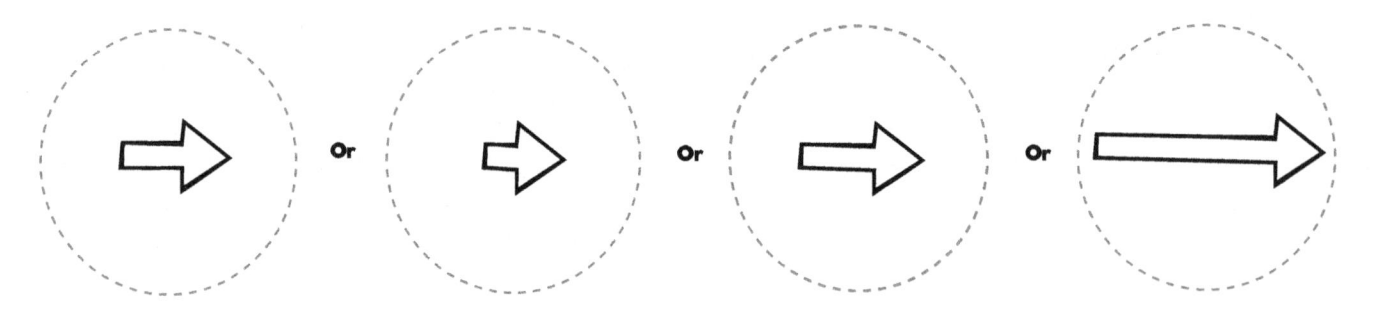

Or   Or   Or

Which pencil is the SHORTEST?

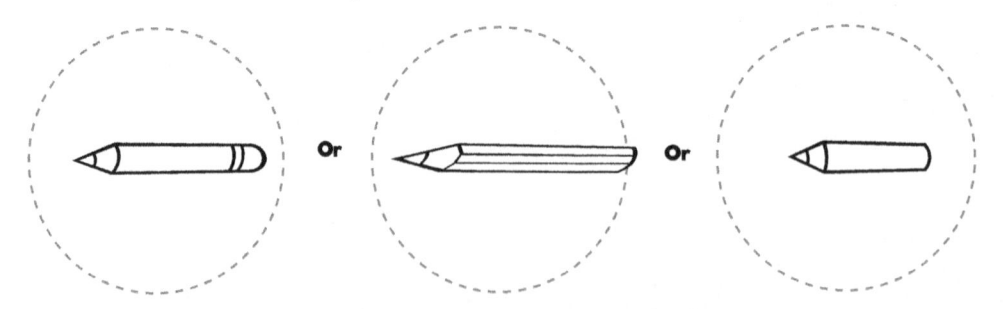

Or   Or

Which arrow is the SHORTEST?

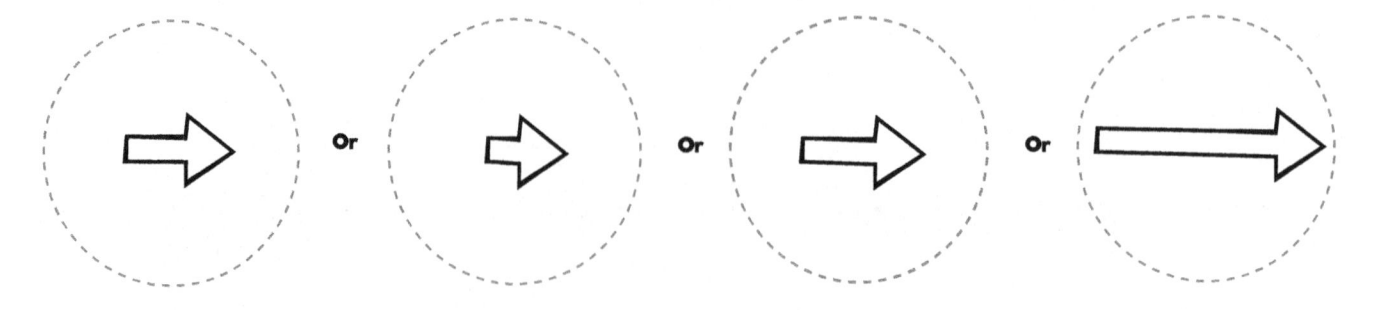

Or   Or   Or

Here is a picture of a snake. Draw and color a LONGER snake here.

Here is a picture of a long fish. Draw and color a SHORTER fish here.

Draw a line here that would be the LONGEST line.

Draw a line here that would be the SHORTEST line.

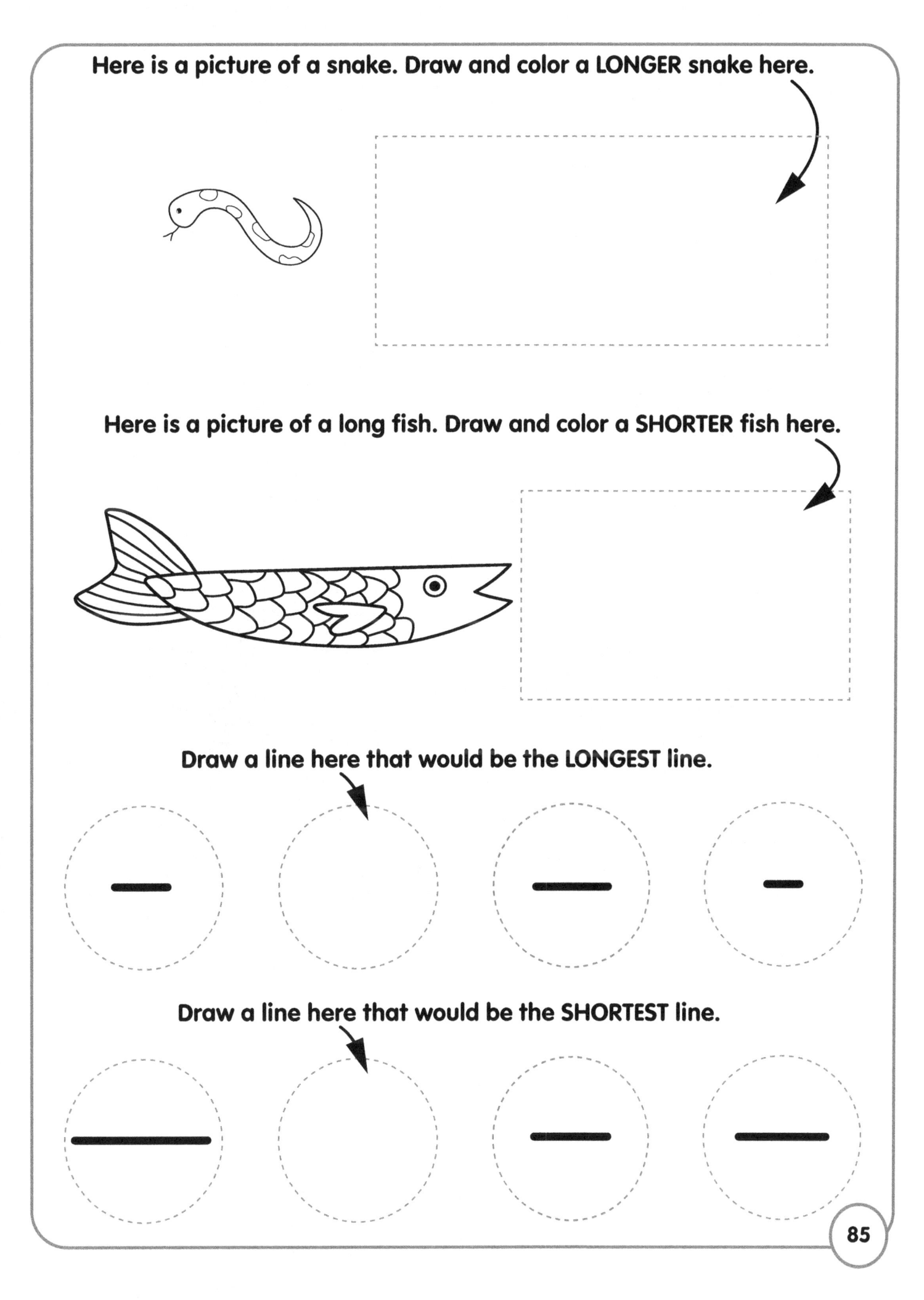

Whole and Half

A **WHOLE**, is one complete thing.

This is a WHOLE pizza.

This is a WHOLE star.

A **HALF** is a **WHOLE** divided into 2 equal parts.

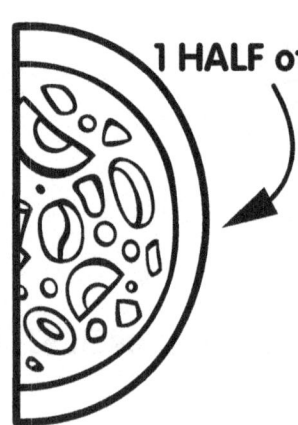

1 HALF of a pizza.

1 HALF of a star.

1 HALF of a pizza.

1 HALF of a star.

1 HALF + 1 HALF = 1 WHOLE

This is a WHOLE circle.

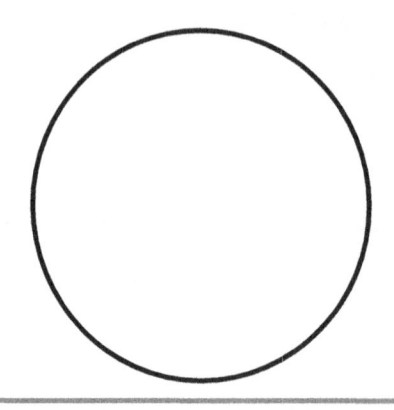

This is a HALF of the circle.

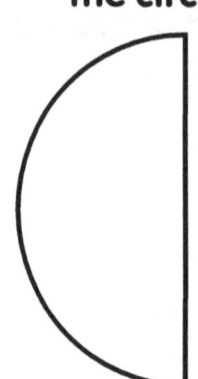

Trace the other HALF of the circle.

This is a WHOLE flower.

This is HALF of the flower. Draw the other HALF to make a whole flower again.

You can also make a HALF from lots of objects, not just one!

Here are 6 stars

You can make 2 halves

How many stars in each half?

_____

Here are 8 leaves.

Draw a line to make 2 halves.

How many leaves in each half?

_____

87

How many circles are there?

Draw a line to make 2 halves.

How many circles in each half?

Here are 6 skateboards.

How many skateboards would be left if you took half of them away?

Draw a line to make 2 halves if you need to.

How many shirts would be left if you took half of them away?

88

What is HALF of 4? ....   What is HALF of 12? ....

Here is one half of a group of triangles.

Draw the other half here.

Here are 6 gifts. Color half of the gifts blue and half of them red.

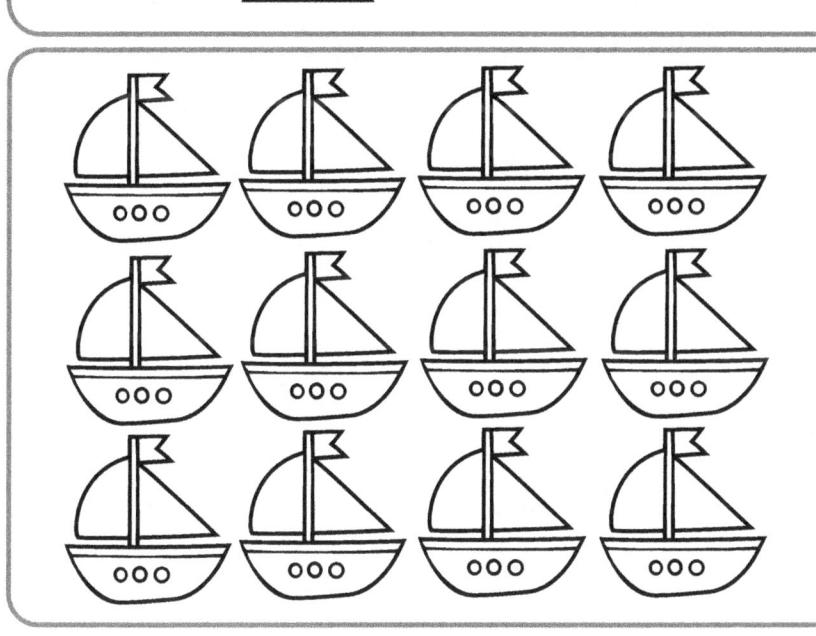

How many boats would be left if half sailed away?

....

....

Telling the Time

Introducing clocks, hours and time

Clocks tell us the time by pointing at numbers.

There are 12 numbers on a clock and each number is a new hour.

A clock has 2 arrows called HANDS. The SMALL ARROW moves slowly and points at the hour, so we call it the HOUR HAND.

If the HOUR HAND points at 6 like this, then it is 6 o'clock.

The BIG ARROW moves more quickly and counts the 60 minutes between each hour. We call the BIG ARROW the MINUTE HAND.

If the MINUTE HAND points straight up at 12 like this then it is a new hour with 0 minutes!

6 o'clock means it is 6 hours and 0 minutes so we can write it like this **6:00**
What time is it on these clocks?

_____ **:00** o'clock   _____ **:00** o'clock   _____ **:00** o'clock

90

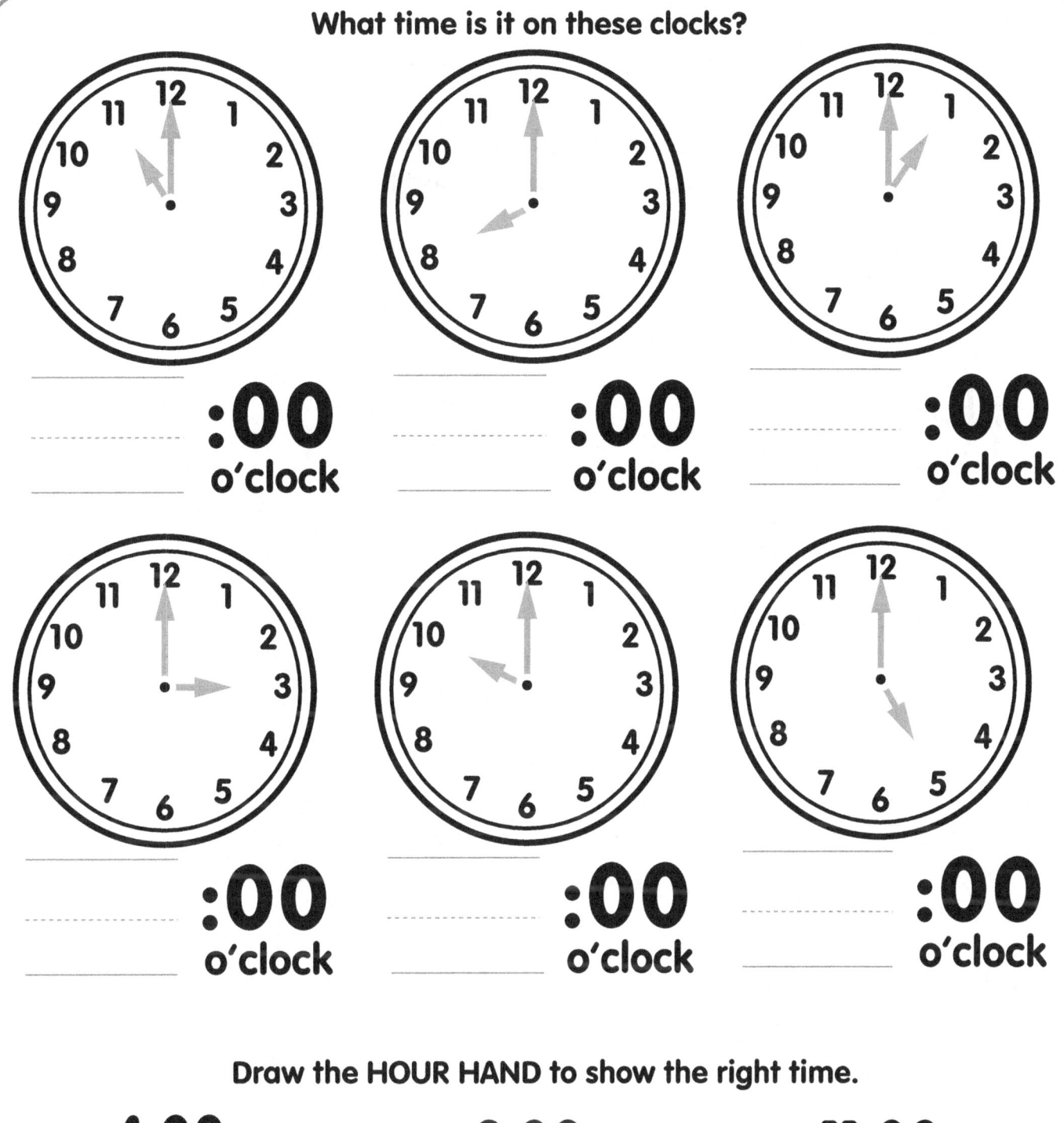

What time is it on these clocks?

_____ :00 o'clock

_____ :00 o'clock

_____ :00 o'clock

_____ :00 o'clock

_____ :00 o'clock

_____ :00 o'clock

Draw the HOUR HAND to show the right time.

4:00

2:00

11:00

91

As the MINUTE HAND moves around the clock we are able to tell the time BETWEEN whole hours.

We can cut the clock up just like a pizza! Have a look at page 86 to remind you about whole and half.

Whole pizza!

Whole hour!
When the MINUTE HAND points up it is a WHOLE HOUR.
This clock shows the time is 9 o'clock.

Half pizza!

Half hour!
When the MINUTE HAND points down it is a HALF HOUR.

The MINUTE HAND has cut the clock in half!
This clock shows the time is half past 9.
The clock is half way between 9 and 10 o'clock.

Circle the correct time shown on the clocks.

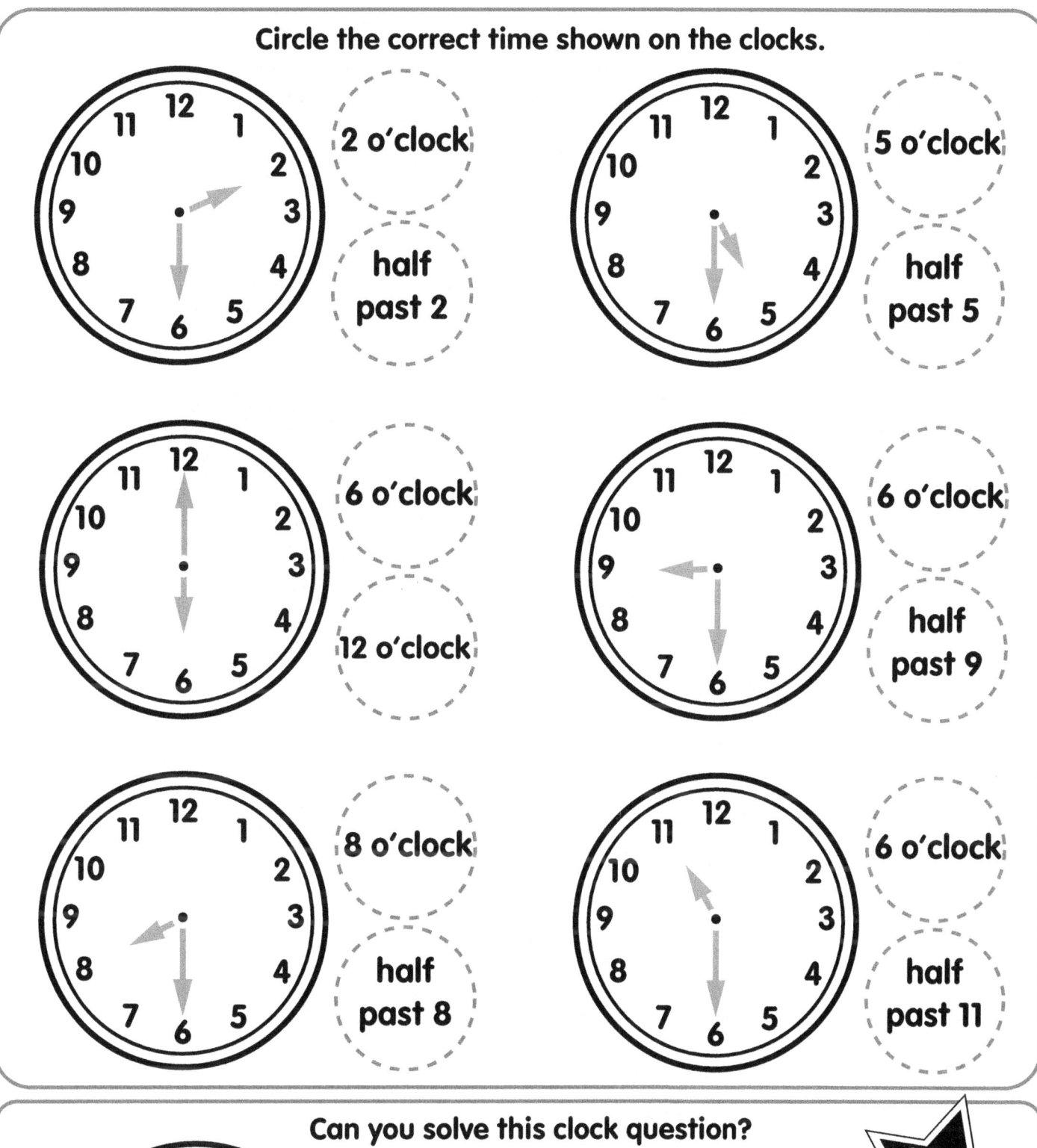

- 2 o'clock
- half past 2

- 5 o'clock
- half past 5

- 6 o'clock
- 12 o'clock

- 6 o'clock
- half past 9

- 8 o'clock
- half past 8

- 6 o'clock
- half past 11

Can you solve this clock question?

If you woke up at 8 o'clock and went out to play 2 hours later, what time did you go out to play?

Draw the HOUR HAND and MINUTE HAND on the clock.

SUPER STAR
CHALLENGE!

93

Challenges!

Combine your Super Star math skills to find the answers

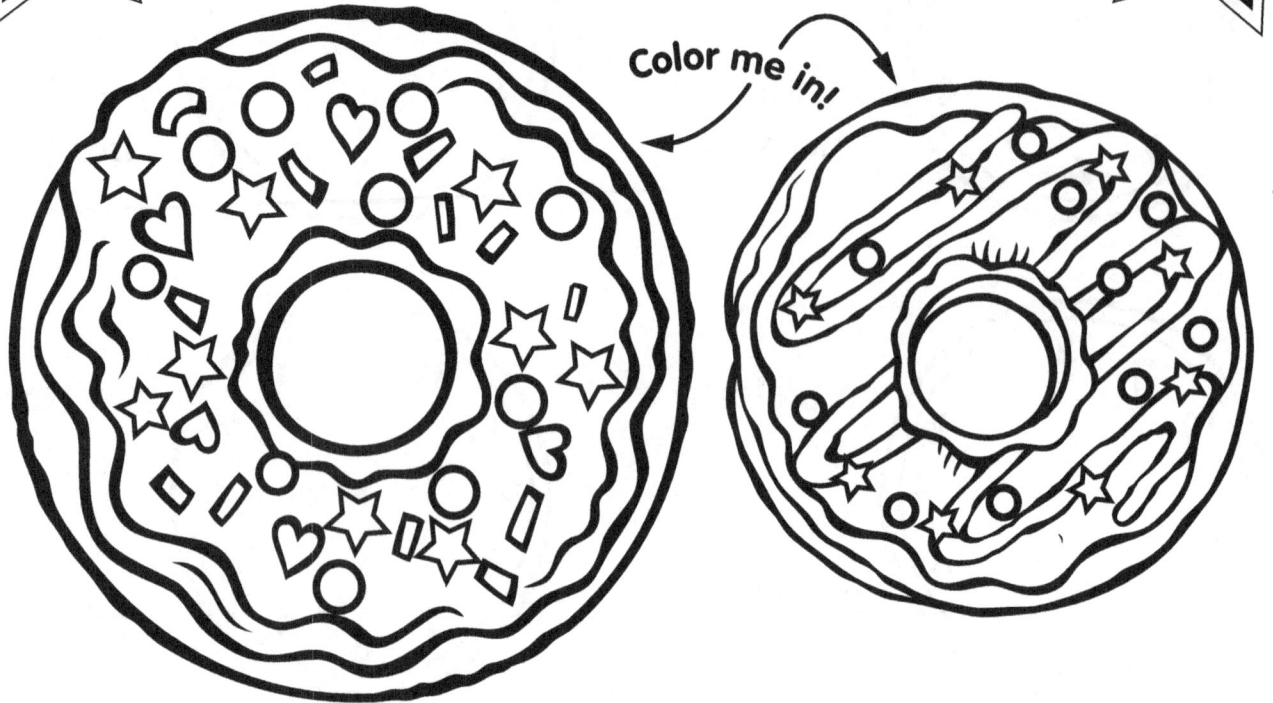

Color me in!

How many donuts are there? _____ Is that an ODD or EVEN number?

Which donut is BIGGER? The LEFT or the RIGHT?

☆ How many stars are there on the bigger donut? _____

○ How many circles are there on the smaller donut? _____

ADD the number of stars on the bigger donut to the number of circles on the smaller donut.

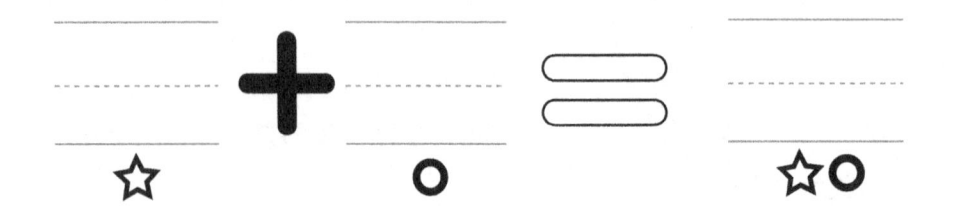

_____ + _____ = _____
☆   ○   ☆○

Color me in!

How many butterflies are there? _____   Is that an ODD or EVEN number?

Which butterfly is the BIGGEST? A or B or C

● How many circles are there on the biggest butterfly? _____

★ How many stars are there on butterfly B ? _____

SUBTRACT the number of stars on butterfly B from the number of circles on the biggest butterfly.

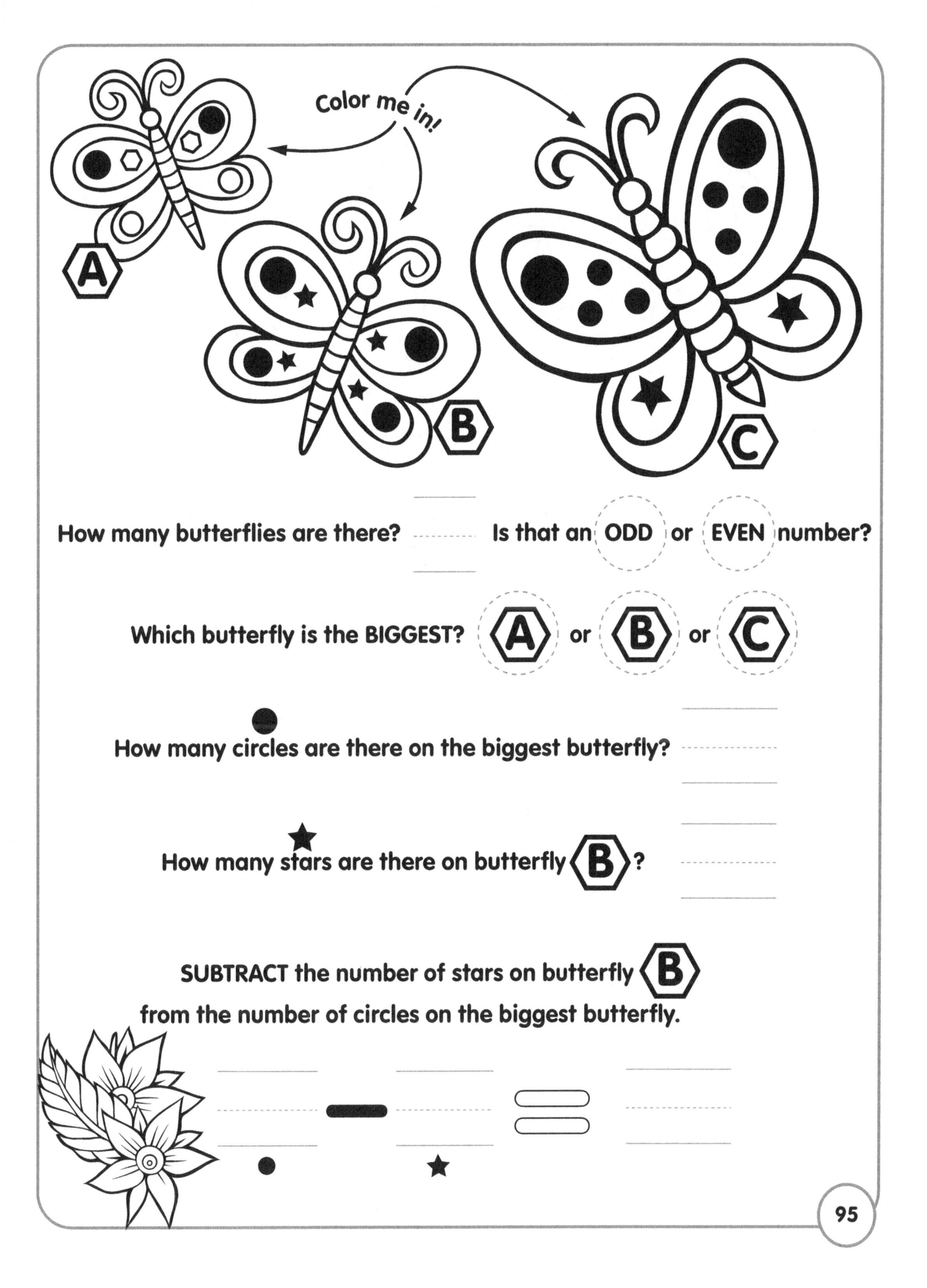

_____ ● — _____ ★ = _____

95

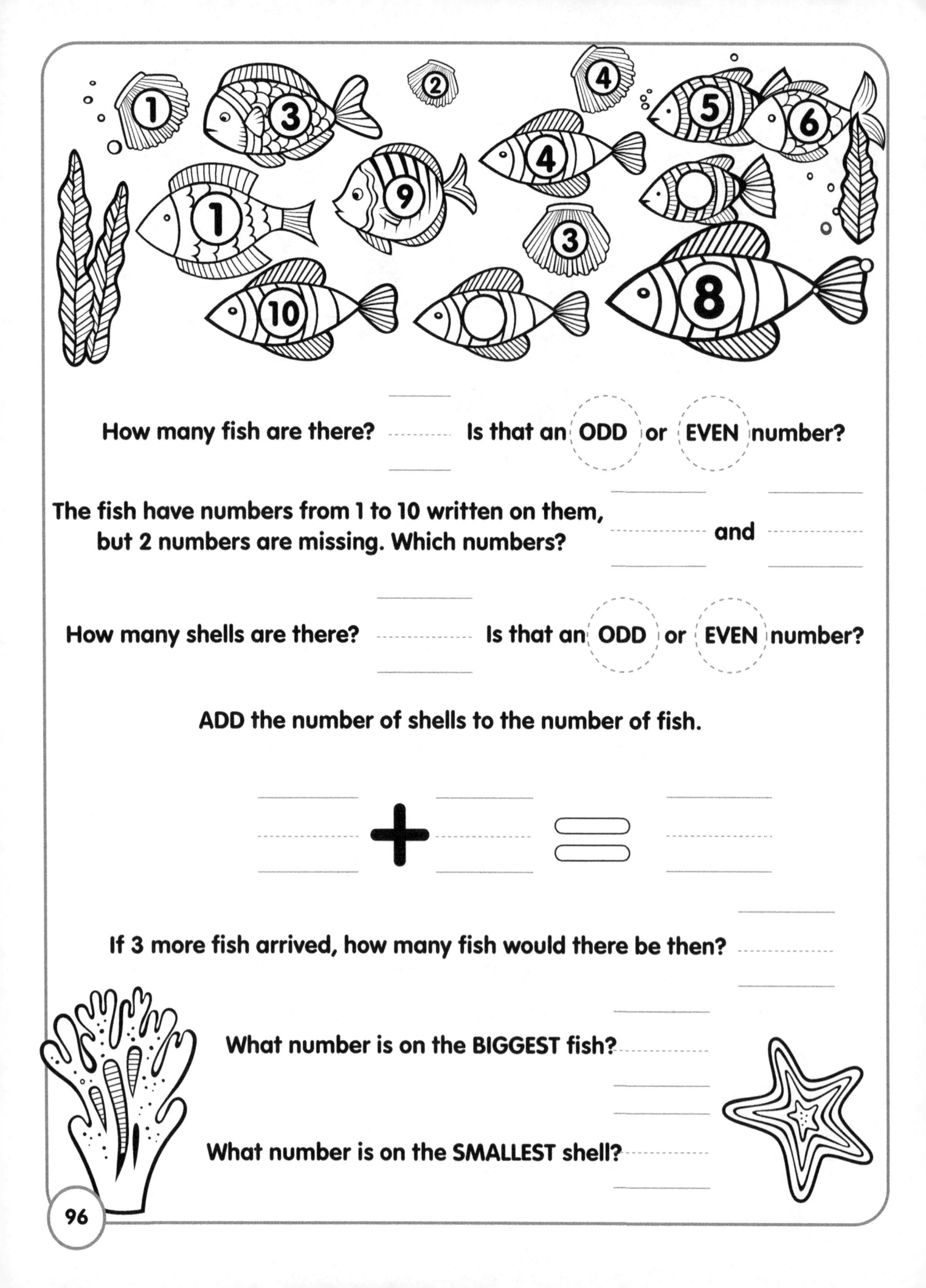

How many fish are there? _____ Is that an ODD or EVEN number?

The fish have numbers from 1 to 10 written on them, but 2 numbers are missing. Which numbers? _____ and _____

How many shells are there? _____ Is that an ODD or EVEN number?

ADD the number of shells to the number of fish.

_____ + _____ = _____

If 3 more fish arrived, how many fish would there be then? _____

What number is on the BIGGEST fish? _____

What number is on the SMALLEST shell? _____

96

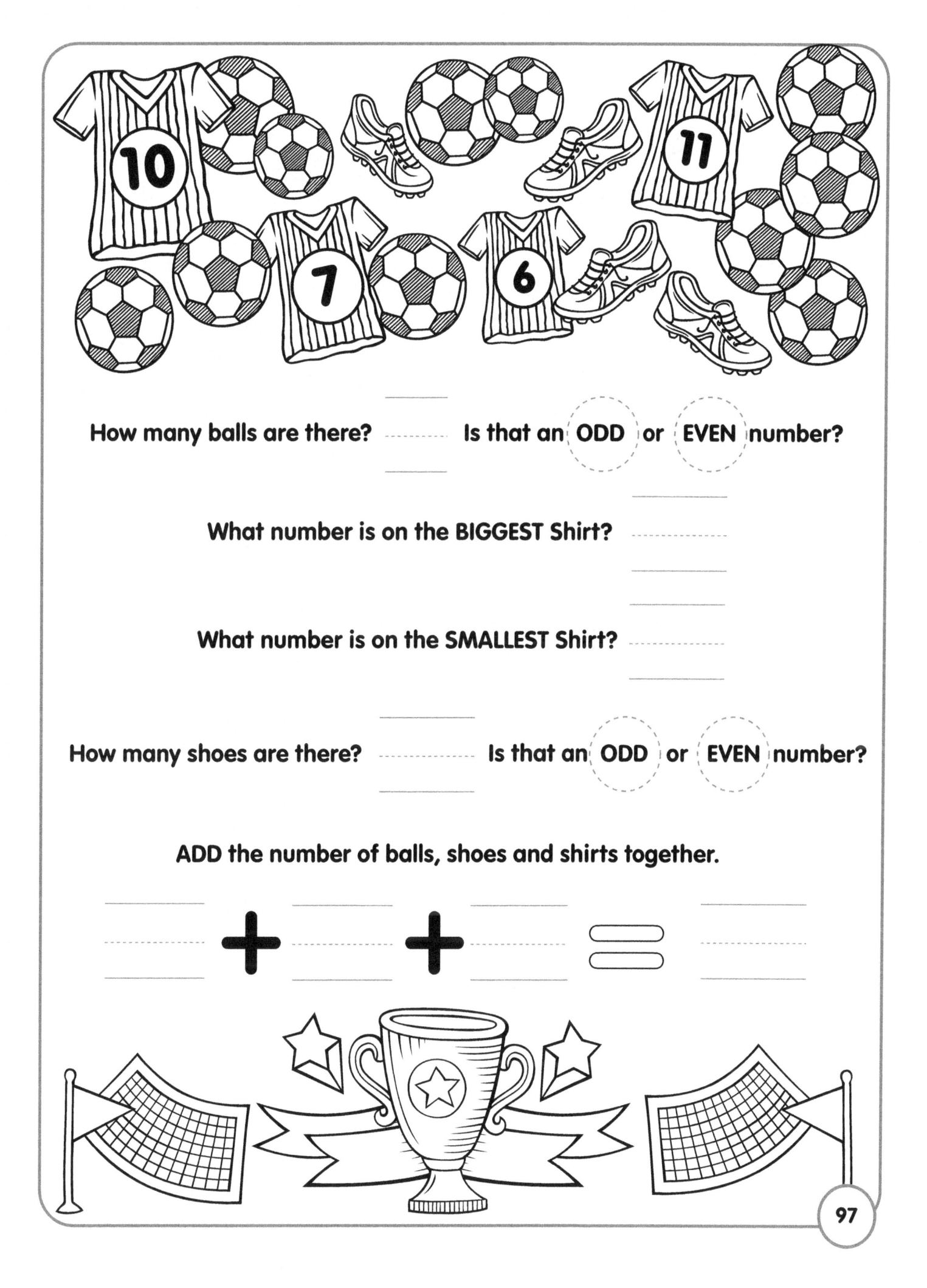

How many balls are there? .... Is that an ODD or EVEN number?

What number is on the BIGGEST Shirt? ....

What number is on the SMALLEST Shirt? ....

How many shoes are there? .... Is that an ODD or EVEN number?

ADD the number of balls, shoes and shirts together.

.... + ... + ... = ...

97

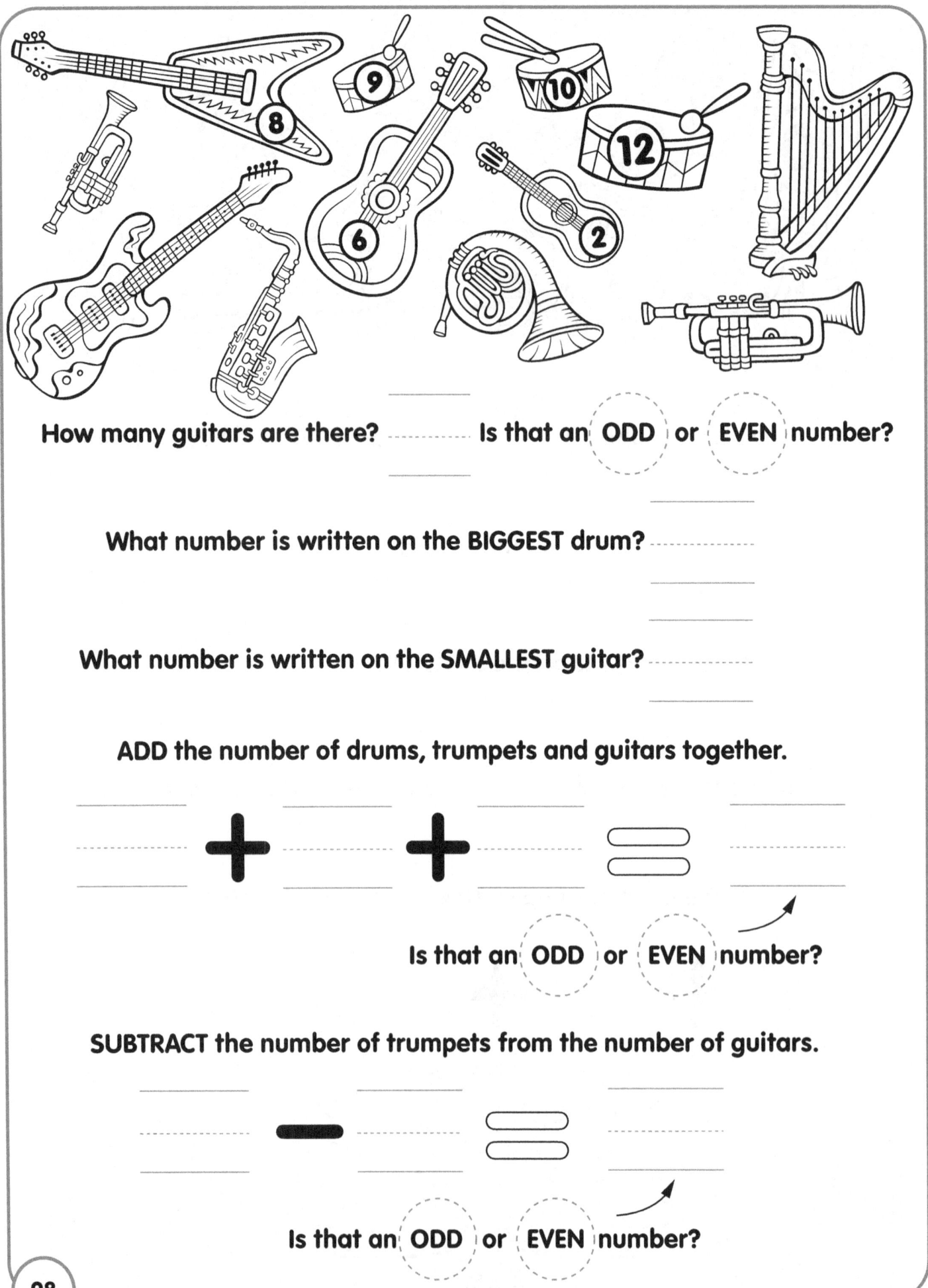

How many guitars are there? _____ Is that an ODD or EVEN number?

What number is written on the BIGGEST drum? _____

What number is written on the SMALLEST guitar? _____

ADD the number of drums, trumpets and guitars together.

_____ + _____ + _____ = _____

Is that an ODD or EVEN number?

SUBTRACT the number of trumpets from the number of guitars.

_____ − _____ = _____

Is that an ODD or EVEN number?

98

Which backpack is bigger?   LEFT or RIGHT

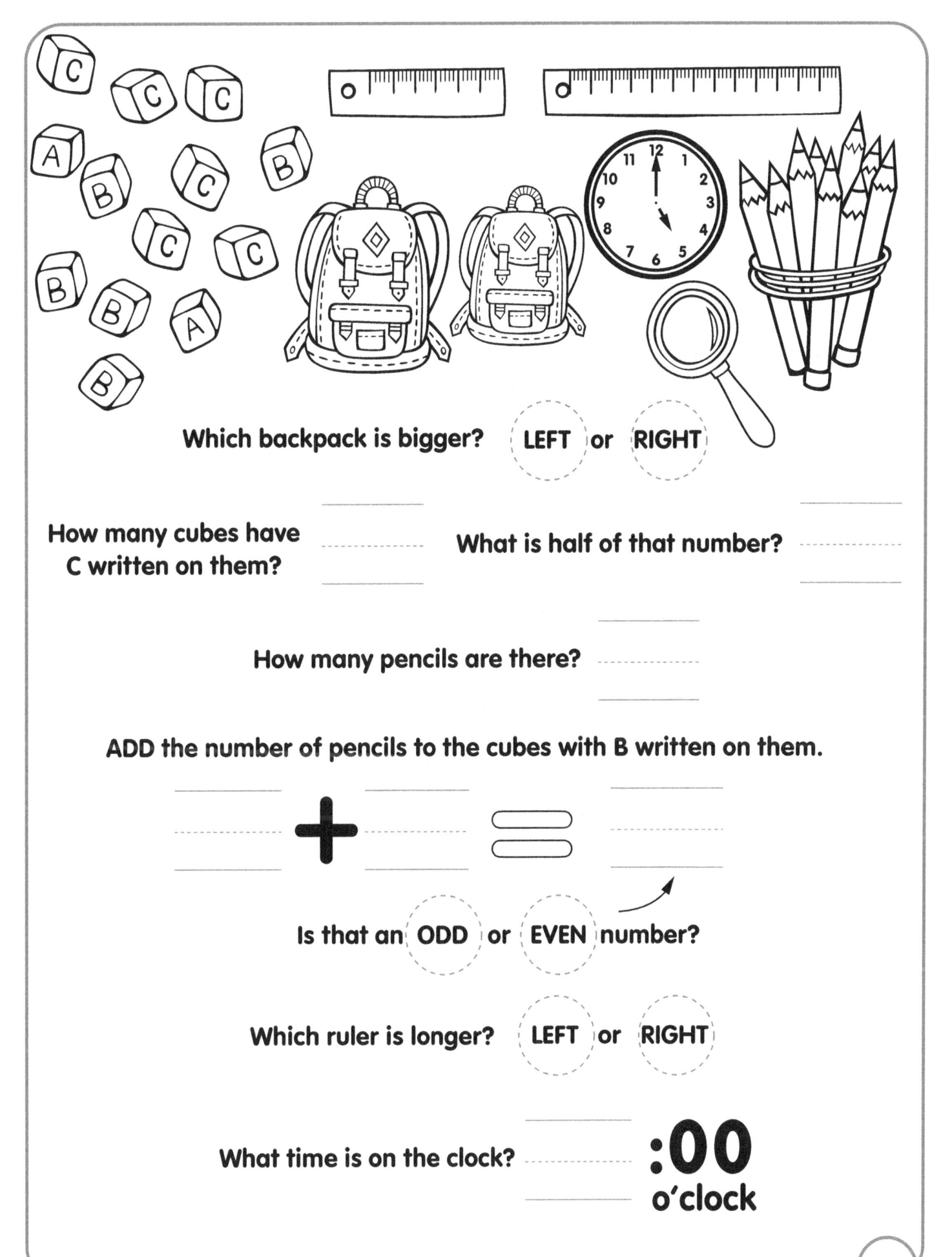

How many cubes have C written on them? _____   What is half of that number? _____

How many pencils are there? _____

ADD the number of pencils to the cubes with B written on them.

_____ + _____ = _____

Is that an ODD or EVEN number?

Which ruler is longer?   LEFT or RIGHT

What time is on the clock? _____ :00 o'clock

Which dinosaur is the longest?   A   or   B   or   C

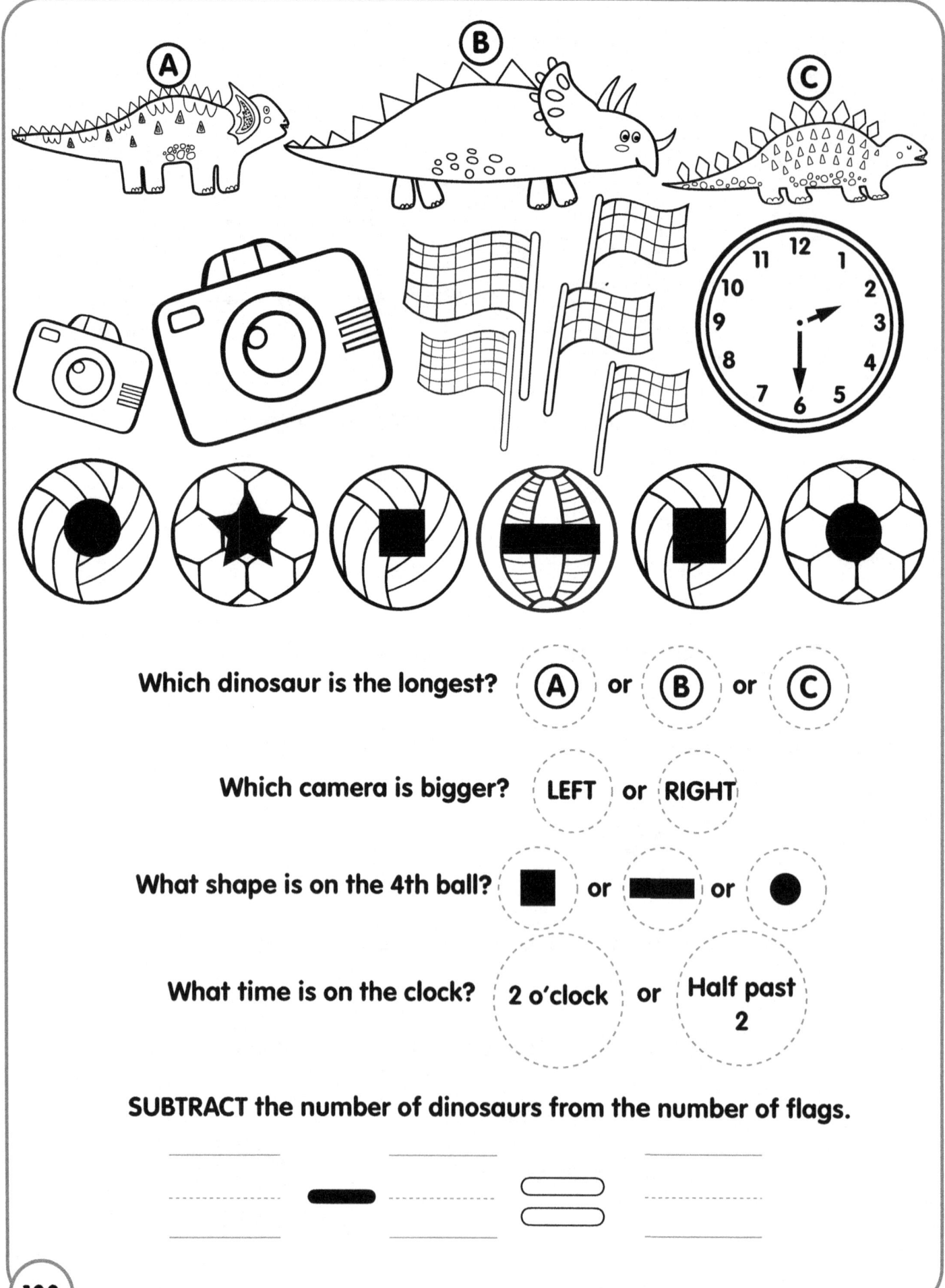

Which camera is bigger?   LEFT   or   RIGHT

What shape is on the 4th ball?   ■   or   ▬   or   ●

What time is on the clock?   2 o'clock   or   Half past 2

SUBTRACT the number of dinosaurs from the number of flags.

Count to 100

Point at each number as you count up to 100!

1	2	3	4	5	6	7	8	9	10
11	12	13	14	15	16	17	18	19	20
21	22	23	24	25	26	27	28	29	30
31	32	33	34	35	36	37	38	39	40
41	42	43	44	45	46	47	48	49	50
51	52	53	54	55	56	57	58	59	60
61	62	63	64	65	66	67	68	69	70
71	72	73	74	75	76	77	78	79	80
81	82	83	84	85	86	87	88	89	90
91	92	93	94	95	96	97	98	99	100

Use this chart to help you whenever you need it.

Color in the ODD numbers red.
Color in the EVEN numbers blue.

Practice Paper

Use these pages if you need space to practice or work out any challenges.

We hope you enjoyed this book. As we learn and grow, we'd love a rating or review for it on Amazon, if you have time. **Thank You!**

Loads more from Under The Cover Press available at **amazon**

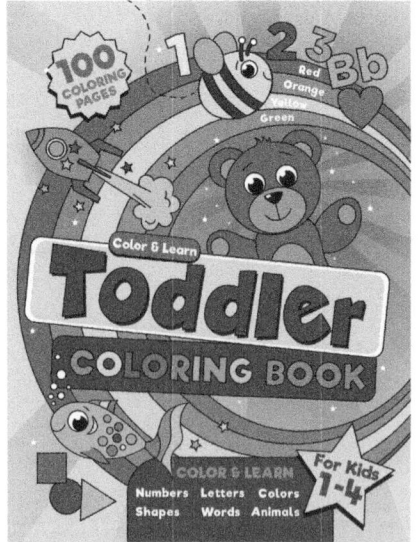

GROWN UPS!
VISIT US AT
UnderTheCoverPress.com
OR SCAN TO VISIT US
FREE STUFF • NEWS • INFO

ISBN 979-8552067565

ISBN 979-8509492808

ISBN 979-8520557715

ISBN 979-8590346219

ISBN 979-8695161878

ISBN 979-8575406419

ISBN 979-8559845876

ISBN 979-8559850436

ISBN 979-8717778565

COMPLETION DIPLOMA

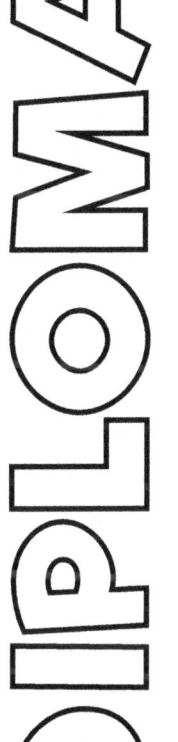

Presented to

For being a Super Star at math!

DATE:

SUPER STAR

KINDERGARTEN MATH WORKBOOK

CUT OUT AND DISPLAY

© 2021 Under the Cover Press. All Rights reserved. WWW.UNDERTHECOVERPRESS.COM
The Right of Under the Cover Press to be identified as the author of this work has been asserted by them in accordance with the CDPA 1988. No part of this publication may be reproduced, distributed, or transmitted in any form or by any means, including photocopying, recording, digital scanning, or other electronic or mechanical methods, without the prior written permission of the author, except in the case of brief quotations embodied in critical reviews and certain non-commercial uses permitted by copyright law.

Although the author and publisher have made every effort to ensure that the information in this book was correct at launch, the author and publisher do not assume and hereby disclaim any liability to any party for any loss, damage or disruption caused by errors and omissions, whether such errors or omissions result from negligence, accident, or any other cause.

This content of this book is presented solely for informational purposes. The author and publisher are not offering it as legal, medical, educational, or professional services advice. Neither the author nor the publisher shall be held liable or responsible to any person or entity with respect to any loss or incidental or consequential damages caused, or alleged to have been caused, directly or indirectly, by the information or advice contained herein. As every situation is different, the advice and methods contained herein may not be suitable for your situation.

Made in the USA
Las Vegas, NV
15 July 2021